A GUIDE FOR
BLENDED FAMILIES

A GUIDE FOR BLENDED FAMILIES

MERGING ASSETS AND NAVIGATING FINANCIAL CHALLENGES

LIFE STAGES FINANCIAL GUIDES

DONNA JEAN KENDRICK

HIGHLANDER
PRESS

CHECKOUT DONNA'S BACKGROUND ON FINRA'S BROKERCHECK

Cetera Financial Specialists LLC, member FINRA/SIPC, is a registered representative offering securities. Advisory services are offered through Cetera Investment Advisers LLC. Cetera is under separate ownership from any other named entity. Sephton Financial, LLC and Cetera are not affiliated.

This communication is strictly intended for those residing in DC, DE, FL, GA, MA, MD, NJ, NY, PA, VA, VT, and WA.

ISBN: 978-1-956442-48-9
Ebook ISBN: 978-1-956442-49-6
Library of Congress Control Number: Applied For.

Published by Highlander Press
501 W. University Pkwy, Ste. B2
Baltimore, MD 21210

Cover design: Hanne Broter
Author photo: Sarah Miller

Ordering Information: Special discounts are available on quantity purchases. **Contact:** hello@donnajeankendrick.com Grief Recovery Specialist®

DISCLAIMER

To my sweet hubby, Jimmy Gehan, and our six little buggers:
Connor, Katie, Squish, Jeanie, Delaney, and Seamus.

CONTENTS

INTRODUCTION

If you have this book in your hands, then you must be somewhere in the process of blending a family. The phrase "blended family" is very general and simply means one or both partners are bringing a child or children into the relationship. Once that basic criterion is met, the resulting blend can have a multitude of configurations.

No matter what configuration you have, there are financial complexities to your relationship. At least one member of the couple is financially linked to others in both a literal and symbolic sense. It would take some superhuman level of stoicism to not experience at least a little bit of tension in your relationship over this. Most of us are not superhuman. We notice that finances are a sticking point in our relationship, and we seriously do not want that to become an ongoing or escalating issue.

I know this feeling. Several years ago, I navigated the difficult financial decisions of widowhood. I recreated my career with school-aged children and took many crucial steps to protect and provide for our family. But then along came Jim, and that changed things. Jim, a divorced dad of three, and I, a widowed mom of three, were given another chance at love. As a financial professional, I understood our need to navigate this coming together of two families with honesty and practical planning. For the sake of our own hearts, and in the spirit of doing the right thing for all of our kids, Jim and I had a series of financial conversations that allowed us to move forward together.

I wrote this book so that you can do the same thing and set your relationship up for success. It's always hard to talk about money, and it's even harder when one or both of you have additional responsibilities to other people. But hard does not mean impossible. This book is intended to be one thing that makes it less hard. In these pages you will find resources for how to get started in your financial discussions. You will find stories that remind you others have been where you are. You'll see examples of steps you can take, and you'll be empowered to strengthen your relationship. You're also going to see the value of compromise, grace, and forgiveness because we've all got baggage.

You could be anywhere in your blended family journey when you pick up this book. You might be just starting to get serious, and you're looking for resources that will help you be proactive about forming a blended family. Maybe you're already blended, and there's a financial disconnect that you just can't get beyond on your own. Or maybe things are okay in the here and now, but you're avoiding conversations about the future that need to be addressed before they become the present. I kept this book short so that you can read the whole thing quickly, and I packed it with helpful tools so that you can revisit the lists and examples as needed.

Throughout these pages, several references will direct you to my website so that you can take advantage of the guides and checklists I reference. These resources are my free gift to you so that you can gain financial clarity in your blended family starting today. Scan the code anytime to visit www.donnajeankendrick.com, where you'll find my friendly face and helpful guides for blended families.

I hope that you find more than financial clarity in this book. I hope you also find relatable, stabilizing guidance. Your family dynamic is unique, but many of the frustrations are common among us, and it often helps to know we're not the only ones who have experienced some of these things. I hope you'll also supply friends or family with a copy of this book when they embark on their own blended family journey. I'm here for you, and I'm here for them. If you need more support, reach out to me at hello@donnajeankendrick.com.

A HOME ALONE

IN MY FIRST BOOK, *A Guide for Widowhood: Navigating the First Three Years*, I shared how I became a widow. I will leave those details in that book and share a summary on these pages. The next part of my story, which I will share more about, is how I became part of a blended family. I want to give you the chance to get to know me a bit. If we ever meet, I want to hear your story, too! There are about a million ways to get into one of these special relationships. I think it's important for us to connect with others with similar—yet very different—circumstances.

One of the things I love most about my work as a financial advisor is learning someone's story. We are not numbers on a page – a series of accounts and values. We're all whole people. We've got battle scars, some healing scabs, and maybe a few open wounds that become part of us. These things don't add or take away from who we are; they just become part of our story, part of our why, and part of our ongoing purpose. My goal is always to see that wholeness, including the scars, scabs, and wounds, when I help people chart their financial plans and goals.

Let's pick up my story right around the time Jim entered it.

A CONTRACTOR'S ADVICE

In the second year after my husband Greg's sudden passing, my kids and I decided it was time for a change. Connor, Katie, James (Squish), and I sold the house, which made us sad due to all the memories interwoven into every room, and we moved into a fixer-upper. Our new house was something we could make our own—a fresh start for new memories.

Like many single moms, I was going through a transition to make sure I could provide for my kids long-term. I had made a workable plan with my financial advisor to ensure that I could work part-time and go to school part-time for a career change. It was busy, but it felt like the smart thing to do at the time.

Our new house needed work that was way above my skill set. My kids and I were fortunate to be surrounded by an amazing support system of family, friends, and neighbors. One of those friends was a contractor named Jim. Jim was a professional carpenter who had put his own career on hold to be the stay-at-home dad for his three young kids. His wife's job provided well for their family, but Jim also enjoyed picking up small jobs in the community to stay busy and keep his skills sharp. He liked helping families like ours who had home projects that could be done over time.

Before you start getting any ideas, let me be upfront that there was no romantic flirtation between Jim and me at that time. He was a contractor I paid to fix things in my home, and our relationship was 100% above board.

That being said, Jim was in my home a fair amount. He saw that I was running myself ragged, trying to work part-time, study all night, be present for my kids at all of their activities, and manage our household.

He finally came out and asked me, "Why are you doing this?"

Blank, slack-jawed stare from me. When you're in the thick of it, you keep plodding forward. You don't think about whether or not there's another way, you keep your eyes on the goal.

But Jim wasn't in the thick of it. He was simply the contractor in my house for two years, thinking I was insane. "Just quit work and go full-time with studying. Just get that done."

"Huh," I thought. "He's probably right." So, I called my financial advisor and asked if I could make it work. It turned out that I could. I had the financial resources I needed to cover one year. If I buckled down and passed my exam within a year, I could start my new career as a CERTIFIED FINANCIAL PLANNER™. So that's what I did. I took advice from my contractor, quit my job, and went full steam ahead at my career change. And it worked!

Dating Fails and New Tries

During that busy time, I tested the dating waters again. Dating after divorce, the death of a spouse, or the end of a relationship that involves children is just plain difficult. There are new vulnerabilities. There is confusion about how to trust and what to share.

I had spent my entire adult life with my late husband. At that point, I didn't know how to "do" a relationship. Unfortunately, someone I dated took advantage of me. In my naïveté, I had shared more than I should have about my finances and career plans. I learned my lesson quickly and recalibrated a bit on dating boundaries.

Jim's story is his to tell (maybe I'll convince him to write his own book), so I will say that his marriage eventually dissolved. He and I continued in the same circles. Heck, he had even witnessed some of my dating fails! He knew that I was cautious.

Eventually, at least a year after his divorce, Jim told me he was interested in dating me. He had been for a while, actually, but he wasn't willing to approach me until he had experienced some financial recovery after his divorce.

The timing was right. Jim and I were both in a place where we were interested in one another, had a good baseline of rapport and respect, and were mature enough to know that it would take some effort to get it right. I said yes to dating, and I'll tell the rest of our story in the following chapters related to blending families and finances.

UNPACK YOUR BAGGAGE

BEFORE WE GET TOO FAR INTO THE GUIDANCE, I WANT TO flesh out the idea of a blended family a little bit. The only defining factor for the purposes of this book is that at least one of the partners in the current relationship has a child or children for whom they are financially responsible.

Here's what this might look like in the real world:

- Two divorced individuals who each have biological or adopted children from their first marriages;
- One childless person and one person with children from a previous marriage or relationship;
- One divorced person and one never-married person, each with children from previous partners;
- One widowed person with children and one divorced person with 50/50 custody of their children;
- One person with full custody of their children and one person who gets their kids one night a week and every other weekend; or
- One person with young children and one whose youngest is about to graduate high school

- Partners who each have children from previous relationships and also share a biological or adopted child.

Does your relationship fit into something that looks like one of those categories? As you can see, you don't have to be a parent yourself at this time. But if you are entering into a serious relationship with someone who is a parent, you are part of a blended family.

By the way, I'll discuss this more later, but I want to be clear that marriage isn't a requirement for being in a blended family or following this book's guidance. What I do pre-suppose for my readers is that you're in a committed, long-term relationship in which each partner's finances will have an impact on the other. I'm going to stick with the word "partner" throughout this guidance in order to generalize all the possible relationship configurations. Feel free to mentally substitute your favorite pet name as we go along.

EXPLORE YOUR MONEY STORY

There is a story behind your relationship with money. It's one that has been forming and taking shape throughout your life. Your history with money goes all the way back to your own childhood. What did your parents teach you? What did you learn by observation or intentional teaching?

How did you personally get money, and what did you do with it? Did you have prudent financial guidance as a child, were you kept in the dark, or did you suffer the consequences of someone else's recklessness?

As you got older, what changed? Did you form new habits, learn lessons from people outside your family, or witness the impact of financial decisions? Have you followed in someone's footsteps, or did you commit to exactly the opposite of your chief influencers?

When did you start earning money? Were you hustling with a neighborhood business at eight years old, walking to work at the neighborhood ice cream stand at fourteen, bussing tables at sixteen, or helping out around the family business from the minute you could walk? Or maybe you stayed out of the workforce during your youth. Some parents believe that school and sports are your jobs until you reach a certain age, so your allowance is meant to be your earnings. I'm sure you've noticed now, as an adult, that conversations about child labor can get very interesting! People have strong opinions about work based on when and how they earned their first dollar. How did you develop your stance on that matter? How did you manage the money you earned, and does that original process still rule your decisions today?

If you were previously married or cohabitating with someone, how did you handle finances as a couple? Were you comfortable with the arrangement? Did you have more or less control or knowledge than you wanted? Did you and your former spouse have a conflict about money, or were you generally on the same page? If you have children, how have your attitudes and behaviors changed since they were born?

I know these are a lot of questions! Don't be overwhelmed. Just like you might tell someone the story about how you grew up and what schools you attended, you will need to tell this story about how you interacted with finances. And just like you might feel some emotions bubbling up when you tell the story of your childhood, you'll probably notice them in this financial backstory as well.

There's a reason I call this baggage. It's unavoidable that emotions are behind your relationship with money. As you recall the important turning points throughout your life up until now, you might notice that you're directing some negative emotions *at* other people. Maybe it's your parents. Their mismanagement of funds took a toll on your social life or your ability to go to a good college. Maybe you are still harboring a grudge against a sibling or a friend who talked you into squandering your savings on something that wasn't worth it. Maybe you're still mad at that first boss who took advantage of your time and never fully paid you what you were owed for your work.

If you're reading this book after a divorce or separating from someone with whom you share a child, there is a whole other list of money hurts you might be harboring to this day. Like I said, money is emotional.

Now it's all well and good if you take an hour to blame someone in your past for failing you somehow. But after your hour, it's time to deal with the facts on the ground as just that. No matter how you have been negatively impacted by your own or someone else's financial decisions in the past, staying in that place of hurt, anger, or fear will not help you accomplish your goals today.

When I was young, my dad was the sole income earner in our home. Although my mom managed the family finances, her name was not on any accounts, and she didn't have any income tax earnings. My parents got divorced when I was a teenager, and she quickly realized that she couldn't establish any credit in her own name. Now, she could be as mad about that as she wanted, but her goal was to get on with her life. That means she dealt with the facts on the ground, did what she needed to do, and got herself a credit history. She put up with a job she hated just long enough to get into one she truly enjoyed, and then she started thriving. Within a year, she qualified for her own credit card, started saving for her own retirement, and learned how to manage her finances. If she had decided to stay mad, she never would have had the right attitude to network and interview her way into the job that would sustain her for the rest of her working life.

It's hard to say if my mom would have done things differently, even if she had known more about credit earlier in her life. The choice to forego income to be a stay-at-home parent is not just a financial decision; it might have been an acceptable trade-off. This is why I don't want you to dwell too much on the past. First of all, you can't change it. Second, there's no way of actually knowing things might have gone another way, even if you had that information back then or if someone had made a different decision. Trade your emotions for the lessons learned and allow that to help you make more informed decisions moving forward.

One client of mine is a first-generation American. Her immigrant parents instilled solid convictions about never being in debt to anyone. They paid for everything in cash, were wary of banks, and taught her to avoid all forms of credit. Needless to say, this was a difficult enough barrier for her to overcome as a young adult who needed credit to rent an apartment or buy car insurance. When she got engaged to a young man who had grown up with no qualms about using credit or carrying reasonable debt, she struggled to accept that he was quite responsible with money.

At first, my client was frustrated that her parents had limited her understanding of finances. But at the same time, she knew that their values had come from a desire to proudly claim their part of the American dream. She knew enough about their home country's culture to consider their financial approach to be a prudent one. She was not about to do a complete reversal and get reckless with debt and spending. Her husband wanted to ensure they could live a comfortable lifestyle within their means but not entirely without debt. They eventually learned to compromise by including payoff timelines (early whenever possible—and making sure it's always possible) in their discussions about large purchases. Looking back, she can certainly appreciate her parents' perspective. She's also doing her level best to raise her own kids with a more balanced understanding of finances so they won't have the same hurdles.

I'm sure you have some significant memories around money that have turned you in one direction or another. As you explore your money story, try to be honest and nonjudgmental. Again, these are just facts. There's no need to be embarrassed about mistakes or overly proud about successes.

EVALUATE YOUR RELATIONSHIP WITH FINANCES

Once you have a clear picture of how you developed your relationship with money, you'll want to evaluate it as objectively as possible. You have given some thought to past influences and lessons. What does all that look like today, in this present moment?

Remember that this evaluation is in preparation for discussing finances with your partner. You're exploring these issues now so that you can have an open and honest conversation about them. With that in mind, think about the following:

- How do you make both small and significant spending decisions?
- Do you prefer spending or saving?
- Do you like to manage money and transactions, or do you eyeball your accounts to avoid overspending?
- Do you trust other people to know about your finances?
- Do you have any big fears about money?
- Do you feel most secure when your finances are under joint control or your personal control?
- Does the word "budget" shut down your brain entirely?

The better you understand how you personally interact with finances, the better you will articulate your needs in the relationship. We've all seen the statistics that finances are one of the biggest topics of conflict for couples. I think this mostly comes down to people not understanding their own relationship with money well enough to identify the disconnect.

What you learn by evaluating your relationship with finances is that your stuff is about you. Now, you can step back far enough to see that your and someone else's approaches are different. You can get humble and collaborative rather than defensive or self-righteous. Don't get me wrong; you can still have opinions about what is prudent or reckless regarding financial behavior. But it's crucial to understand your own thought processes and behaviors before you try to learn about your partner's.

I mentioned that someone I dated took advantage of me. Frankly, I was too open and honest about finances with this person because I didn't know any better. I had been married my whole adult life, so I didn't quite understand the concept of boundaries and protecting my privacy in the dating world. After that experience, let me tell you, I learned fast.

When Jim and I began dating, I had walls up. Of course, Jim had known me as a friend, so he knew a fair bit more than a stranger might. But I was guarded for sure, and I was hesitant about progressing our relationship because of it. I didn't want to be taken advantage of again, so I was more inclined to continue dating while maintaining separate lives. Jim, on the other hand, was interested in marriage. If we were going to move in that direction, I was going to have to confront my own history and emotional connections with money first. That was the only way I could come to the table, ready to move to the next step as a couple.

NO JUDGMENT

When you closely examine your relationship with finances, it's easy to fall into a place of self-blame and embarrassment. Let me stop you before that happens.

Guess what? You're human!

This exercise is not about giving yourself a grade. You're just collecting information so that you can make decisions moving forward. The more honest you are with yourself, the better prepared you and your partner are to face the future together.

One of my clients came to me after she had been divorced for about five years. Her ex-husband was a debt spender, meaning he used credit cards for everything and never paid much more than the minimum payments. This had really turned her off to using credit cards because she hated constantly having so much debt hanging over her head. She had a few credit cards that she rarely used. She had gotten them early during the divorce process to cover minor expenses while she got set up on her own. But she practically had a physical disgust reaction to using them. She paid them off as fast as she could and allowed them to gather dust in her wallet. When she got a letter that one of the cards would be canceled for being dormant for so long, she reached out to me. She was nervous about losing her credit history but didn't want to fall into that old debt-spending pattern. She was saving to qualify for a mortgage, so she was both spending-conscious and credit conscious.

When we reviewed her accounts, I was able to point out that she had a credit card with a nice "cash back" feature. We discussed strategies for using that feature to her advantage, such as buying gas and groceries on the card and paying it off monthly. Over time, she would accumulate those cash back rewards to use towards large purchases, travel, or to take as a credit on her account sometimes. Or, she could put a larger purchase on the card and commit to full repayment over a few months. Her concerns about getting into debt had come from her disdain for old spending patterns, and she was carrying around an all-or-nothing perspective. That perspective is just information. It's not something to judge or to hold as virtuous—it was simply a financial behavior she practiced.

We used that information to come up with a new perspective on credit. Once we explored some ways to manage debt as part of her affordable financial plan, she felt empowered rather than afraid. She already had her eye on some patio furniture, so she decided to buy the set on her credit card. Then, she committed to paying off the balance over the next four months so that the interest would be minimal. We set up automatic bill payers timed with when her income was direct deposited so that the process would be seamless. She continued saving for her mortgage with strategic, rather than fear-based, financial decisions.

Unpacking your own baggage around finances can be humbling and a little bit uncomfortable. But at the end of it, the goal is that you have gained an understanding of your decision-making processes and attitudes towards money. Being humbled by our own stuff helps us get in the right frame of mind to open the door to our partner's side of the equation.

OPEN THE DOOR

ONCE YOU MAKE IT THROUGH THE HARD WORK OF evaluating your own relationship with finances, you're in a better spot to meet your partner where they are.

If you're reading this book, then I don't need to tell you that blended family relationships are prone to tension. I mean, all relationships have tension. But by definition, blended families have more people involved from day one. And those people will always have an impact.

With that in mind, this chapter is intended to help you remove some of that tension before you and your partner come to the financial table. Remember, our goal is a healthy financial future for both of you, as well as for the people you're blending into your relationship. If you've been playing either offense or defense up to this point, it's time to get back on the same team.

ACCEPT THE PAST WITHOUT JUDGMENT

Just like you, your partner has a lifetime of experiences and lessons that have led to their current money mindset. They have their own childhood, family dynamics, and other influences that have shaped the way they make decisions about saving, spending, credit, debt, and wealth.

If your partner was married or a contributing member of a household, they will come to your relationship with that baggage. If your partner has children, they might have some financial obligations that can't be managed in a different way.

Just like with your own financial history, everything your partner has in their history is simply information. Today's reality is unaffected by how you judge the decisions and events of the past. They simply exist. All you can do is decide how to move forward from this moment.

If I was going to move forward in my relationship with Jim, I knew that I had to take down some of those walls I had built up from past relationships. But I also knew that had to be a two-way street. If I was going to let him in a little, he had to let me in a little. I needed to know where Jim was coming from financially.

I found out that Jim actually had a few of his own walls up. My walls were up out of protection. Jim's walls had more to do with avoidance and having been caught unprepared. The avoidance was just his personal style. He doesn't love working with numbers. Well, not in the financial sense, anyway. Jim is a hands-on tradesman. He knows everything there is to know about numbers when he's measuring for new cabinets or rewiring a ceiling fan. But balancing the checkbook and calculating IRA contributions? That was not his thing.

Jim was happy to have his first wife manage their family finances while they were married. Upon moving out of his marital home, Jim was caught unprepared when he discovered that he immediately lost access to all of his credit and bank accounts. He was in a very tough spot of starting over from almost nothing. He was hesitant to share with me that there was a point when he was living on canned green beans until he could regain some financial footing. He realized in retrospect that he should have opened up his own bank and credit card accounts earlier to avoid that level of financial hardship. He still would have been broke, but only in the way that a lot of divorced dads are at first. He had all the raw materials to recover. But he still had the walls up.

Between his general dislike of working with finances and his sensitivity to sharing just how tough it had gotten for him at one point, he would have preferred to avoid the whole discussion. If I was going to get what I wanted, which was to open our respective financial books and figure out our future together, I needed to reassure Jim that I accepted his situation without judgment. It was just information, after all. And the only way we could move forward positively was to get it all on the table.

When you and your partner decide to be on the same team, it's easier to accept each other's current financial reality exactly where it is right now. This allows you to get into a future-focused frame of mind where you can make plans and financial decisions together to benefit your blended family.

CONFRONTING IMBALANCE AND UNFAIRNESS

Because blended families come in all different configurations, there's usually some noticeable imbalance in financial responsibilities.

For example, when a thirty-year-old who has never been married and is childless meets a divorced parent of two elementary-aged children, there is a huge disconnect in how each partner has been making financial decisions up to this point.

A common blended family scenario is when two divorced people with children have different custody and child support arrangements. Stereotypically, the woman might have 70% of the parenting time with her children and receive child support. Meanwhile, the man gets his kids one night a week and every other weekend and pays child support. When you add in expenditures for time in the shared household, different arrangements for extracurricular activities, and other lifestyle expenses, the money coming in and going out can be really unequal for each partner.

In my case, I was a widowed mom of three, and Jim was a divorced dad of three. I was the sole earner for my kids, but we did have some death benefits that factored into our household income. Jim, on the other hand, was in a standard divorce and child support arrangement. I was the only decision-maker for my kids regarding finances, and he was co-parenting.

I recently spoke to someone who got married to a divorced dad with two kids right around the same time that his ex-wife had two more children with her new husband. The ex-wife decided to leave the workforce until her two youngest kids were ready for school. For about five years, three adults contributed income—dad, stepmom, and the ex-wife's husband—but the one who had become a stay-at-home mom seemed to be unilaterally making all the financial decisions. And boy, did she enjoy signing the kids up for all kinds of activities and coming up with reasons they needed money from Dad. Stepmom told me it was frustrating, but she loves her husband and his kids. The financial strain wasn't the kids' fault, and she wouldn't allow it to impact the relationships in her home.

Any blended family could have a large disparity in income or wealth, debt, expenses, or lifestyle. A parent might have a different philosophy about spending and saving than another parent or a childless member of the couple. Parents who pay child support versus those who receive child support might have strong opinions about this obligation. Ex-spouses or co-parents might have some level of control over one partner's spending habits.

At the end of the day, it might seem unfair. It will probably be imbalanced. And you definitely won't agree about everything. These are the facts on the ground. So, what do we do with them?

BAKE THE HUMBLE PIE

If you don't want to get locked into a power struggle for the life of your relationship, my advice is to get humble. You and your partner are a couple of flawed individuals who are both doing your best to make a life together.

Whether one or both of you are bringing financial complexities into the relationship, your goal is to move forward as a cohesive unit.

Go ahead and take another hour to be mad or frustrated about the most painful parts of this situation. By the way, I recommend taking this hour alone. The intention is to ventilate your feelings so that they dissipate and disappear.

If you decide to unload on a friend or family member, that person might form a permanent opinion about your partner. Now, someone has a bias against your partner that will inevitably cause problems down the road.

You know what I mean if you have ever faced this situation. Has your mom ever called when you are annoyed with your partner, and you made the mistake of venting to her? Now, the next time you all get together, she's shooting passive-aggressive daggers on your behalf when you got over the whole thing weeks ago!

If you really want to get it out of your system, here are some ideas:

- Write a letter, then burn it;
- Drive to the beach, woods, or mountains and just scream it out alone in your safely parked car; or
- Speak to a professional counselor, but make it clear you need to pour it out and never bring it up again.

If you can manage to work through this frustration alone, it can't come back to haunt you. When you're done, it's done. Give your partner a big kiss, and let's get to work.

COME TO THE TABLE

Now that you've really set the table for productive financial planning in your blended family, it's time to sit down together. Don't put the pressure on yourselves to handle all of the information and planning in one conversation. Sometimes we need to come back to the table a few times with cooler heads, fresh ideas, and compromise in mind.

This phase is where I do recommend working with a third party. A financial advisor is a neutral person who can help you and your partner go through the information with clarity, and maybe a little less tension.

I recommend doing a bit of research to find an advisor who is a good fit for both you and your partner. Consider working with a Certified Divorce Financial Analyst®, which is a financial professional who has engaged in specific training to make sure divorced clients consider the future impact of their financial decisions. These professionals provide guidance and advice that is unique to scenarios involving divorce.

Other questions you may want to ask your potential financial advisor include:

- Will we meet directly with you, or will you assign us to someone in your office?
- Are you available for in-person, phone, or virtual meetings during evening or weekend hours?
- What are your fees and what services do you offer?
- Are you a CFP®, CDFA®, or other type of credentialed professional?
- Are you a fiduciary?
- How robust is your referral network for things like Real Estate Agents, insurance agents, attorneys, and accountants?

Of course, one of the most important factors in choosing your financial advisor is what your gut says. You and your partner absolutely must both feel comfortable with the professional you choose. In that case, you'll never be fully honest with someone you don't like or trust, and you'll certainly never make real headway on your goals. Only move forward with the financial advisor who is the right fit for both of you. See the resources section of this book for links to a guide on identifying the right financial advisor for you and your partner.

My own style is to be a handholding, high-touch advisor. Most of my clients are in a sensitive place, and they need someone who spells out all the steps and assignments (I give homework!) but who is also very compassionate and patient. I'm not the right advisor for everyone, and that's okay! That's why you and your partner need to interview and get a feel for your potential advisors.

I am honored to work with all of my blended family clients. They have no obligation to choose me, so I take my clients' trust very seriously. As a CFP®, I am a fiduciary. That means I am bound by law to always act in the best interests of my clients rather than my own. This information helps a lot of clients feel more secure in providing all of their financial information to their advisor. They can set aside their concerns that the advisor is more focused on their commission than on providing advice in the client's best interest.

When preparing to meet with a couple, one of the first things I do is ask them to complete a financial virtue survey, which tells me how each partner makes decisions. You can access this survey on my website by visiting the Resources section of this book.

This survey allows you and your partner and your financial advisor, if you're working with one, to see each other's value system around money. Everything I mentioned previously about unpacking your own baggage regarding finances bears out in the results of this survey. But now you can look at each other's financial virtues side-by-side and see how they are similar and different.

I didn't have this survey yet when I first asked Jim to sit down with me to discuss our finances. Boy, do I wish I had! At the same time, I don't think he would have liked it very much. He prefers to live for the day, keeping a loose eye on the accounts. Jim's ex-wife had a background in accounting and lived for planning how to save and spend. Now there he was, looking at me, a widowed mom who became so focused on financial security that she started a whole new career in financial planning—and he has to reckon with someone who keeps track of transactions again. Poor Jim.

We didn't tackle it all at once. Our process was more of a series as we worked through the relationship and came to terms with what the other was looking for. Jim was focused on marriage. He liked being married, and he wanted that permanence. I also liked being married, but I had competing interests. Because of my status as a widow, there were issues that would impact my kids' and my finances if I remarried. There were also emotional worries on my end. I've shared about my mom having to recreate herself financially after my parents' divorce. But that's not the end of the story. She also remarried rather quickly, which she later admitted was for financial security. It didn't end well, and she went through what I call a "gray divorce" again later while in her seventies. I didn't want to get remarried out of fear. But I also didn't want to avoid marriage out of fear.

For me, marriage had to be a wise financial decision. How romantic!

I can joke about it because we did have our romance. But in all seriousness, I needed a well-rounded relationship. Once I trusted Jim and committed to where our relationship was headed, I tended to over-share information about my financial values and history, particularly the financial practices in my marriage. I wanted Jim to understand where I was coming from financially. I felt that the best way for us to succeed in remarriage was to be financially equal, even if our income itself was not equal.

TO GET MARRIED, LIVE ENGAGED, OR COHABITATE

From a purely financial perspective, there are various pros and cons to getting remarried or blending your family without marriage.

Marriage is an institution, so it comes with legal strings attached. These strings might significantly impact each partner and any kids involved. Here are a few things to consider:

- **Alimony or Spousal Support.** Remarriage typically brings an abrupt end to alimony or spousal support that is being paid to you by a former spouse. My mother found this one out the hard way!
- **Pension.** A widowed spouse collecting their deceased spouse's pension may or may not lose those benefits upon remarriage. My late husband worked for the government, and his pension was important to our family income. I would lose this benefit upon remarriage, so I needed to make sure I could replace it before I got remarried.
- **Social Security.** A widowed spouse who waits until after age sixty to remarry can still collect their deceased spouse's social security. I lost my claim to Greg's benefits when Jim and I got married. Social Security has other technicalities regarding divorce and remarriage, so it's important to understand how it will impact your retirement years.
- **Employer Retirement Account Beneficiaries.** If you have a 401(k) through your employer, your spouse is the default

beneficiary, even if you have other beneficiaries listed on your account. For blended families where one person would prefer to have their funds paid out to their children or someone else, a special spousal consent form must be on file.

- **Health Insurance.** If you are divorced or widowed, access to your health insurance will change upon remarriage. In my case, I would lose access to Greg's health insurance, even though I was paying for it out of pocket. It may be worth reviewing all of the available health insurance plans to see if moving the kids' coverage to someone else's plan will be financially beneficial for everyone.

- **Financial Aid.** When aspiring college students apply for the Federal Application for Student Aid (FAFSA), the calculation is based on their primary household income. A single parent's income will produce a much different federal aid allocation than a remarried parent's household income.

- **Tax Implications.** There are tax credits and deductions that depend on your filing status. Consider these changes before you get a big surprise from your accountant at tax time.

- **End of Life Decisions.** While it is easier these days to legally designate your end-of-life decision-makers, marriage automatically confers some rights. I mentioned in my first book that my maternal grandmother, Babci, and her beloved partner, Al, never got married. Even though she was his life partner and the person who cared for him during the end of his life, she had no legal rights to make the final decisions for his funeral, burial, or obituary.

- **Wills and Estate Planning.** Since a spouse is the automatic next of kin, partners with children from previous relationships need to discuss the path of inheritance. Countless books, documentaries, movies, and everyday conversations relay the drama around this hot-button issue regarding remarriage.

These issues will have a different impact on any given couple. For some couples, marriage is the priority, so all of these financial and legal complexities have to be worked through, whatever the consequences. Some couples value the practicalities more than marriage, and so they may decide to live engaged or cohabitate without a definition, either permanently or until all the kids are launched.

I personally could have lived engaged indefinitely. I recognized several benefits of delaying marriage for each of us and all of our kids. Jim was a no-go on that. Marriage was his priority. He was willing to delay long enough for me to accomplish some of my goals, such as replacing Greg's pension with my own income and getting a health insurance plan under my company name.

What worked for us was to set a timeline. I like to work backward from deadlines. For example, I signed up for a marathon once because that was the only way I would be motivated enough to train for a marathon. So that's what we did in our relationship. We set a wedding date—two-and-a-half years away—that would give me time to plan for all the financial changes. Once we set that date and made it public, I was on the clock.

Jim was truly gracious about my need to get all of our ducks in a row, and he was satisfied knowing we had a date. When I look back at the timeline and all the requirements I put in place for us, I feel like I overcomplicated it a bit. Despite that, I think that our mutual respect for one another's sensitivities and priorities set a crucial foundation for our marriage.

Some couples might prefer to look forward to each benchmark. Once one task is accomplished, you set the next one and work towards that. This strategy often works for couples focused on reducing their personal debt before they are willing to merge their finances. They are focused on the end goal but give themselves plenty of wiggle room to reach it so that there's less pressure. My caution on this approach is that you both really have to be comfortable with how long it could take. If it turns into a stall tactic for one partner, that's a communication and commitment issue.

I'll go into more detail in a bit, but if debt reduction is a top priority, listen to my podcast about pulling your credit report by visiting the Resources section of this book.

DETERMINE PRIORITIES, NEGOTIABLES, AND NON-NEGOTIABLES

Whether or not you plan to get married, if you are blending your family into one household, you will make joint financial decisions most of the time. This is why coming to the table to discuss finances is so important.

Once you each complete the financial virtues survey, you'll better understand how you each make financial decisions. Next, you'll review and discuss all of that and start deciding how you'll make these decisions as a couple. Remember in the last chapter how I went on at length about setting aside all judgment for your own and your partner's past? That's going to be key to these sets of conversations. It's also why I highly recommend getting a professional to help you!

Very few couples are entirely in sync about how to deal with money. Sometimes, we have one saver and one spender. Sometimes, we have the thrifter versus the high-tech shopper. Sometimes, both people are savers or spenders, but they value what's worth saving for or spending on differently. These differences shouldn't be a problem as long as you can get them on the table and communicate what will work best for the relationship. You each have strengths that will benefit the financial aspects of your future together. We just need to identify them, figure out how they work together and balance each other out, and put them into action.

One of the first things worth discussing is how fully you want to merge your finances as a household. Once upon a time, it was a downright scandal for spouses to keep personal checking or saving accounts that the other could not access. With the rise of divorce, remarriage, non-married cohabitation, and all other types of relationships, separate accounts are more common. In fact, I work with first-time marrying couples fairly often who want to keep separate personal accounts.

The most common arrangement is that each partner has their own personal account, and then they share a joint account. We even call it a "house account" these days. They might have both a joint savings and a joint checking so that they can each contribute to covering the bills and making sure they have enough for holiday shopping, vacation, and emergencies.

My personal opinion is that everyone deserves some privacy. If I want to buy Jim a gift, I should be able to use a credit card that gets paid out of my personal checking account to truly surprise him. At the same time, there are some things that maybe we want to be accountable to each other about. For example, since we both buy groceries and grab meals on the go for ourselves and the kids, we should consider keeping all of that on the joint credit card. That way, we can review it once in a while to ensure we're being reasonable about our transactions.

Speaking of the kids and the financial plan, how will that work in your blended family? You may both be coming to the table with preconditions about how you use or intend to use money for your household kids. Some financial obligations are court-ordered and not even up for discussion. Others may be based on values or affordability. If child support is a factor for either of you, keeping separate accounts might feel more secure because of periodic reviews of that calculation. Realistically, a new spouse's income should not impact child support calculations, but it is something people tend to worry about.

Beyond court-ordered spending on kids, how do you each feel about spending on extras? Do kids need to get a part-time job in high school to pay for certain things? Do you intend to pay for college, weddings, house down payments, or family vacations? There might be a lot of variances in how you and your partner feel about these things. It can be really tough to work through the reality that the way money is allocated among the kids might never be truly fair or equitable. There are other households in the mix, two different histories of lifestyle, and financial values that all come into play. As I already mentioned, the kids will also be impacted financially by your choice to get married or remain unmarried when it comes to financial aid and possibly their inheritance.

Because the financial discussions involving the kids of your blended household can be particularly touchy, it's also really important to decide what can be discussed directly with them. Don't forget the complicating factor that there might be another parent whose discussion of financial matters is out of your control. You and your partner need to be unified on this front to maintain the appropriate level of financial privacy over your relationship.

I like to break down all of these financial categories into a play on the concept of *yours, mine, ours, and theirs:*

- **Yours and mine.** These are your and your partner's separate finances over which you each retain your own personal control. Property, investment accounts, heirlooms, or cash might come in under these headings.
- **Ours.** This includes all of your joint finances moving forward. It can include your joint or house bank and credit accounts, co-owned property, retirement and investment accounts, and everything else you are co-mingling in the relationship.
- **Theirs.** This encompasses the finances for the various children involved in your blended family. The money that is allocated for them for now and for the future based on court agreements, personal values, family circumstances, and original savings will all impact your overall household finances.
- *Theirs.* These are the other folks who impact your blended family finances. Ex-spouses, ex-in-laws, family of deceased spouses, and even half-siblings of other families may have some financial role in the kids' lives. You may never get all of the relevant information about those funds, plans, or

obligations. Still, it's essential to remember that the kids in your blended family are being, or will be, influenced by it at some point.

With all these realities in view, it's time to look at the actual numbers on the page. You'll determine your net worth as a couple so that you can take all of that financial virtue information and put it into action for the operation of your household.

DETERMINE YOUR HOUSEHOLD NET WORTH

Taking control of my finances was so much of a priority when my late husband died that I recreated my whole career around it. Being thrust into such a vulnerable place so suddenly made me acutely aware of my need for financial awareness. I was very fortunate to find a trustworthy financial advisor in my first year of widowhood, and that experience inspired me to become the person I needed in those early days. Once Jim and I started planning to blend our families, I discovered the need for financial planning services for families in transition. I broadened my scope of practice to continue being the kind of advisor I have needed in my own life.

If you want to jump ahead, visit the Resources section at the end of this book, which has a link to all the free resources mentioned in this book.

Couples blending a family often come together with financial hurt, embarrassment, insecurities, anger, or damage. It's not easy, but these discussions are necessary if you want to set this relationship up for open and honest financial commitment. In my practice, I do all of this groundwork and guide those conversations with the couple from the beginning. That way, we can get beyond the yuck and muck with as little emotion as possible.

Ready or not, it's time to buckle down and look at all the numbers. I use an eight-stage process for financial planning that is offered as a guide by the CFP® Board. My process looks a bit like this:

1. Understand the blending couple as individuals and as a family to learn about what they are confident in, as well as their frustrations, concerns, fears, and challenges.
2. Identify and select the goals the couple must address now and those that can wait until later.
3. Analyze the couple's current financial options and what they want to accomplish together.
4. Develop financial planning recommendations to help them accomplish short-term and long-term goals.
5. Present the recommendations to the couple in a way they can easily understand and help them create a plan of action.
6. Implement the plan of action according to a timeline, and work as a team to stay on task.
7. Monitor the plan for progress and to provide additional support and communication on an ongoing basis.
8. Add a little love because this is really hard work.

CASH FLOW

To get started, you will need to look at your cash flow. Where do you both have money coming from, and how do you spend it? Essentially, what does it cost to be you on a daily, weekly, monthly, and yearly basis? If you're still in the planning phase of blending your family, you might each need to do a separate cash flow worksheet. One might be enough if you live together and share household expenses. I have a grid already set up for you to use for this process, and you can access it from the Resources section of this book.

1. Once you have the worksheet, pull out yellow and blue highlighters or crayons and a pencil.
2. Fill in all the information you know off the top of your head, then take a break.
3. Set aside some time to gather all of your important papers and accounts into one spot, or pull them all up on your computer and sit down with your worksheet again.

4. Update any information from Question 2 that you can verify and highlight those lines in yellow. Leave information that still needs verification unhighlighted.
5. Highlight the blank lines in blue and take another break.
6. Reach out to your accountant or payroll administrator at work to fill in some of the blanks.
7. When you and your partner complete your respective (or joint) worksheets, take them to your financial advisor to start the next steps.

Just writing all of these numbers down can be intimidating. Add to that sharing them with your partner and advisor, and you might feel a little bit of panic setting in. Don't go down that road! As I keep saying, this is just information. The numbers are a starting point for heading into a financially productive and secure future in your blended family.

If you're not a big fan of paper, pencil, and highlighters, you have many other choices. If you are most comfortable in front of your laptop or desktop computer, you can create this entire worksheet in your favorite spreadsheet platform. Or if you prefer app-based tools that you can use on your phone or tablet, your app store will offer several options.

To evaluate the different apps, run an internet search for "best budget apps." Financial websites like Nerdwallet and CNET will have comparison articles. Some of the features they will review include:

- Zero-based budgeting, which allocates every dollar, versus envelope budgeting, which puts all of your money in different spending "envelopes."
- Apps that synchronize with your bank accounts versus manual input apps that rely on you to input information.
- Free apps versus paid subscription apps.
- Apps that allow you to include investment information versus apps that limit your input to cash.

If you need time to determine what is best for your financial situation, take advantage of free trials before committing to a paid subscription.

CREDIT REPORTS AND SCORES

While we're already talking about gathering together the numbers you would rather no one else put eyes on, I might as well let you know that you will need to print out your credit report. Your credit report summarizes how you have managed various debts and credit accounts over your lifetime. A credit report used to be an elusive document. These days, you have all kinds of access to it. At the very least, you are entitled to a free annual credit report from each major reporting agency at www.annualcreditreport.com. There are three credit bureaus for the United States: Equifax, Experian, and TransUnion.

If you didn't listen to my podcast about pulling your credit report yet, this is a good time to circle back to it. Visit the Resources section of this book for all the resources and links mentioned.

Your other account providers might also offer credit reports and scores anytime you want to review them. Credit card companies and banks have started keeping customers informed about their credit and the factors that impact it through monthly notices.

If you haven't reviewed your credit report in a long time, or ever, review the first section carefully to make sure all of the information is accurate. As you continue moving through the report, you'll find a list of your accounts, history of late payments, judgments, and the amount of credit available or debt owed on each account. Check closely for incorrect information so that you can report it to the agencies. You might find some very old accounts that you forgot you had, so you'll need to consider whether they should be closed or kept open for maintaining your history. Your financial advisor can help you weigh the pros and cons of keeping or closing each account.

Your credit report will also show you anything that you own jointly with another person or are listed as a co-signer. If you share accounts with a previous partner, or you have co-signed loans for your children, it will all be in the report. This is a good time to make a plan for removing yourself or an ex-spouse from accounts that should no longer be shared. Depending on interest rates, balances owed, and other factors, this might not be a quick fix. Speak with your financial advisor about how to go about this, especially if communicating with the other person named on the account is difficult or contentious.

Jim had to work with his ex-wife to remove her name from the title of his car, which involved selling the car to the dealership, buying it back as a used car, and paying all the transfer taxes again. His ex-wife, on the other hand, really wanted to maintain her low interest rate. Jim agreed to keep his name on the car until it was paid off. Once she held the title, they met at a notary to remove him from it.

Finally, your credit report will show you who has checked your credit history in the past two years. If you have applied for financing for a car or a loan, you'll see the credit checks. Too many checks on your credit can pull down your FICO score, so keep that in mind. After the death of a spouse, divorce, or separation from a long-term relationship, credit is sometimes the only way to make sure the ends meet for a time. It's tempting to look at easy credit as the fastest way to get back on your feet, but there are always tradeoffs.

Your FICO score, which stands for Fair Isaac Corporation (the software that calculates the score) is a number that reflects the compilation of your credit history. This score is not part of what you can receive for free through www.annualcreditreport.com, but it may be easy to view on your credit card or bank website. This number can be anywhere between 300 and 850, with most Americans averaging just above 700.

If your credit score is below 620, you will have a tougher time getting approved for credit or loans. For many of the blending families I speak to, this is a reality. When someone in the couple has had to unravel from a marriage or a shared home, take on all the new expenses of child support, self-support, and legal fees, it takes a huge financial toll. Many people have had to fund their and their families lives with credit during divorce negotiations or while waiting for the life insurance payout of their deceased spouse. When we use more credit, even if the bills all get paid on time, it shows up in the report as "credit utilization." High balances could also still be hanging out there, and there might be a few late payments. All these things can cause a score to drop.

You may already know that your credit report will not be pretty. That's okay! Just print the darn thing out, flip it face down, and slide it across the table, eyes averted. We need to review the facts so that we can formulate the next steps. Bad credit, even terrible credit, can be fixed once we know what we're dealing with. It might take time, but I promise that the satisfaction of seeing a Good or Very Good FICO score is always worth it.

CALCULATING NET WORTH

We looked at cash flow and credit, but there are some other elements of your net worth that need to be reviewed. Your net worth is the calculation of everything you own minus everything you owe. With cash flow, we covered your income and expenses so that you know what's happening day to day or month to month.

Net worth is comprised of all the assets that have accumulated outside your cash flow. This inventory includes real estate property, retirement savings, investment funds, permanent life insurance, valuable possessions, businesses you own, and cash savings.

There is a link in the Resources section of this book to a Net Worth tool.

Similar to the cash flow worksheet, you and your partner should complete it individually if you still need to merge your household. Even if you have brought all of your assets together, it is more prudent to figure out your individual net worth rather than to determine one as a couple.

Something widespread with blended families is that not all of your assets will be equally divided later in life. If you are currently co-parenting minor children, perhaps you'll want the other parent to receive your life insurance proceeds to continue caring for the kids. Your partner might have family property that will pass down to their kids instead of you. You will have other beneficiary considerations if you have new children in your blended family.

What this really means is that your net worth as individuals will not usually blend perfectly into your net worth as a couple. Some assets may possibly always remain in the **Yours, Mine, and Theirs** categories of your long-term financial planning. When I review net worth with couples who are blending a family, we spend a lot of time going over the near and far future plans for their individual net worth assets and their assets as a couple.

One issue that I took care of before Jim and I got married, but after we started sharing a home together, was to name him as the guardian of my kids and beneficiary of my life insurance policy. Several years before, I had designated my best friend as their guardian, but he was now the other primary adult in their lives and would be the right person to continue supporting them.

However, I wanted to use other elements to my net worth to provide for my kids. I wanted to be able to allocate what I believed was their dad's share of my net worth. For example, the house that Jim and his kids would move into with us was the one I had bought with the sale of our previous family home. I felt that the right thing to do was make sure that property would be passed down to my kids if I should die. But I wasn't about to let my little buggers put Jim out on the street if I passed suddenly! I also felt that he had a right to continue living in the house that he was making into a home with me for as long as he wanted. For this and other reasons, I asked for a prenuptial agreement (prenup) and updated my will.

PROTECTING YOUR NET WORTH

I know that the term "prenup" is supercharged with all kinds of emotions. People have strong feelings about these documents, and that's okay!

What I want to share is why writing a prenup for my marriage with Jim was important to me. I had already faced the most unexpected and impossible tragedy. My late husband's death taught me that I am not in control of the future in any way, shape, or form. I love Jim with all my heart, and I want this to be my lifelong marriage. But I am acutely aware that I do not have full control over that future.

Out of that awareness, I wanted to take a few steps to protect my kids for the long-term. I want to protect Jim's kids as well. As blended families, we should be aware that our kids have specific rights to what comes from their own family lines. The prenup is essentially a will for our marriage that is meant to protect the "heirs" whether the marriage ends by death or divorce. If something were to happen that causes the end of our marriage, Jim and I (and our heirs) will be able to part ways with assets that protect each of our own family interests.

There are many reasons people don't like these agreements. Some say that a prenup is basically planning for divorce. Some think that it means you are starting the marriage without trust in your partner. Others say it means one or both partners value money more than each other. One of the biggest objections to prenups is that they always seem very imbalanced. One side feels that they have the most to lose should the marriage fail, so they request the prenup in order to protect their personal interests.

I look at it as a mutual protection document. I want both people in the relationship to come to the table with the intention to remain whole even if the marriage does not. It's not a matter of taking back from the marriage whatever was yours when you came into it, although that can be part of the agreement. It's taking a long-term view of the relationship, determining what each of your contributions make possible for the household, and dividing things fairly based on that.

For example, I have an investment property in the Pocono Mountains in Pennsylvania. Of all the places on earth, it's my favorite. Our prenuptial agreement states that if Jim and I get divorced, he takes ownership of the Pocono house. The house I bought before I first met Jim, the same house that Jim and his kids would move into before we got married, would continue to be my house and then my kids' house. But Jim was always going to have a home. No matter what happens in our relationship, Jim was integral to helping me get my career up and running. He supported me through many goals, loves my children, partners with me in my business, and is my best friend. He is also the other significant financial contributor to our household. Even though I purchased both real estate properties, Jim has earned his share of our life.

The other significant reason I wanted a prenup was to provide airtight clarity for both of our families. The prenup spells out exactly what our intentions are for our kids. My kids didn't have another parent, so if I were to die before Jim, this is how I could protect their assets and provide for them in the way that I had always intended. Jim and I actually came together with different ideas about how we each want to support our kids later in life, so writing those intentions into our document is one way to protect each of our relationships with the other's children.

This is all part of the emotional quality of money in your relationship. When I sit down with clients, we make a visual map of all the accounts. I can see the numbers on the page, but I ask them to talk to me about what it means to them and what they want to see happen with it. By understanding each other's intentions for the assets you're bringing into the relationship, you can come to a wonderful place of respect and appreciation. Believe it or not, a prenuptial agreement *can* strengthen your relationship!

To prove it, I'll share with you that one aspect of our agreement is the succession of my business. Jim is set up to inherit the value of this business, because he has been so important to its development. We may make adjustments as all the kids grow into adulthood, especially if any of them show an interest in joining us. But for now, the value of my practice goes to him if I can no longer operate it.

Prenuptial agreements are not the only way to navigate these decisions. If you are already married, a postnuptial agreement is possible. But then there is also your will and estate planning. You can work with a lawyer to determine the best course of action in providing for whatever comes after your relationship. If you don't have a lawyer who works in wills and estate planning, your financial advisor is a great first step for a referral. These two professional sectors cross paths quite a bit, and your advisor should be able to recommend an attorney who fits your personality well.

MAKING JOINT SPENDING AND SAVING DECISIONS

Now that you and your partner have all the finances on the table, it's time to decide how you will make decisions as a couple. I previously mentioned that you and your partner have a lot of freedom in merging your everyday accounts.

Hopefully, the work up to this point has cultivated a feeling of trust and honesty. The numbers are known, the emotions behind the numbers have been shared, your future hopes and dreams are clear, and past hurts from other relationships have been set aside. It's down to the two of you and how you want to manage your blended household.

Your individual financial virtues will help you determine each other's strengths. It might be very clear that one of you should manage the savings account with an iron fist, while the other handles the grocery, gas, and shopping funds with a slightly looser grip. If you are both big spenders or thrifty savers, your financial advisor will be crucial to helping you find a good balance for money management.

This is the conversation in which you'll want to set clear boundaries about how you each deal with money regarding the other stakeholders in your relationship. Because there are kids and co-parents that are one person's responsibility, not every decision can be made as a cohesive unit. But every financial decision does have an impact on the whole household, so it's necessary to manage them as respectfully as possible.

I understood that it was important to Jim that he and his ex-wife should discuss financial decisions about their kids privately. Jim made parenting a priority, so even though money was never his favorite topic, he took it seriously as an important part of raising children. Sometimes, there were items he discussed with me before finalizing, and other times he moved forward in agreements with his ex-wife and filled me in later. I respected his choice to handle it that way, and I supported his decisions.

That is not to say that I always *agreed* with his decisions, of course. It's very easy to criticize the way one's partner makes financial decisions with their co-parent. I urge all of my clients to exercise all the empathy they possibly can in these moments. When we're not in the financial conversation, we don't have all the details. We also don't have the emotional ties, parental convictions, and motivations that our partners have. It took a lot of frustration and practice, but I finally learned that it was best to keep my opinions to myself.

If I was really struggling to understand a financial commitment he made, I asked him about it from a place of curiosity, not criticism. "Why did you agree to that" can sound like a question or an accusation. When I was careful of my tone and asked it as a genuine question, Jim was much more willing to tell me all the factors that went into the decision so that I could see the full picture. Those kinds of conversations kept us on the same team. He was doing what he had to do for his kids, and I was supporting him.

When there is a sizable difference in how child support and spending contribute to one set of kids over another or one of the partners is childless, there might be some glaring disparity in how money is allocated. The bottom line is that it will probably never be completely fair or equal among everyone in the family. This is one of those things that may never fully resolve, but hopefully, everyone can come to accept over time.

SPENDING DECISIONS

What you will have more ability to resolve is how you make household spending decisions. Here are a few things to get the conversation started:

- What is our personal purchase maximum before we need to discuss it?

- What are the parameters around buying home décor, furniture, appliances, and fixtures with or without input?
- How often should we eat meals out with the kids, without the kids, with some of the kids? What about takeout and fast food?
- How will we plan for holiday shopping, vacations, and birthdays?
- Do we need to set a per person clothing and shoes spending limit?
- Can we afford sports, instruments, hobbies, and clubs for everyone?
- What can we each spend on the joint credit card for lunch with a friend, stopping for coffee, or frivolities?

"I don't want you to ask me about what I spend on coffee," was a specific comment Jim made when we discussed what to spend on our shared American Express card. It sounded like such a trivial thing, but I could tell that he was really serious. I asked him to tell me a little more about that.

While working as a contractor, Jim sometimes worked with other guys and would pick up an extra cup of coffee for them on the way to the job. He told me that his ex-wife got credit card alerts for their shared card, and she once asked him why he had bought two cups of coffee that day. The memory came up when we were discussing our own spending plan. If we were to have a shared credit card, he wanted us both to have some autonomy in how we used it.

We agreed to a $300 alert setting that we both received for our shared American Express card. Jim can buy coffee for a whole crew, and I won't notice unless I dig into the bill.

Once you set some ground rules, see how it feels for a few months. I recommend revisiting it every few months for the first year to see how you're both doing. If you need to recalibrate to resolve some disagreements or tension around how each person spends money, the numbers will still be right there in front of you.

SAVING FOR RAINY DAYS AND EVERYTHING ELSE

Your household cash reserve is incredibly important. Unlike your long-term assets and retirement savings, this is your rainy-day fund. It's money you need to make ends meet if the bottom drops out of your financial security all of a sudden.

I recommend getting at least three to six months into a liquid savings account. By liquid, I mean it has to be money that you can withdraw in cash quickly and without penalties. There are great interest bearing money market accounts that will allow your reserve to build up on its own. But a plain old bank savings account will also work.

We will head back to your cash flow worksheets to determine what's needed for your cash reserve. How much money do you absolutely need to pay the rent/mortgage, keep the lights and heat on, buy food, and cover the bare necessities? That's how much money you and your partner must save for unexpected emergencies. You need three months of coverage in the cash reserve if you each earn a steady income covering nearly half of the household expenses. If you only have one primary income earner or one of you has a highly variable income, get six months into the account.

Your cash reserve needs to be an off-limits account. If one of you is more of a spender, those funds can be very tempting. But you need to set up strict rules over it. These are some examples of acceptable withdraws from this account:

- Major car repairs;
- Loss of income or job;
- An emergency flight to visit a dying or very ill close family member;
- Recover from a natural disaster or fire; and
- Bridging the gap for a leave of absence or job change.

When you need to use money from that account, your first priority after recovering should be replenishing it so that it's available for use next time.

The stock market impacts my income as a financial planner. Jim and I both earn our household income from this business. If the stock market has a huge dip, so does our income. Therefore, we might need to use our cash reserve to stay afloat for a few months.

When one of my clients found out that her dad had a terminal cancer diagnosis, she came to me to say that she wanted nothing more than to spend time with him and her mom. We looked at her cash flow, net worth, and cash reserve to see how long she could afford to leave work to be with her parents. With a few cuts to her expenses, she had enough to cover about five months away from her job without dipping into any tax-qualified retirement accounts. She took a leave of absence and focused on caring for her parents while her dad declined. Her dad passed away after two months. Because of her careful planning, my client still had several weeks to help her mom get through the next steps and take her time getting back to her own life. Her cash reserve made all the difference in allowing her family to spend that precious time together. As soon as she got back to work, she focused on quickly replenishing her cash reserve so that she was ready for another emergency.

Now that we know what the cash reserve is for and why it needs rules, we can move on to other savings accounts. Here's where you can have some more fun. In fact, you might call this savings account your "Fun Money" account or "Opportunity Fund."

This savings account can be treated with a lighter touch than your cash reserve. In this account, you're saving up for large purchases, vacations, major gifts, and planned upcoming expenses. This is where you might be saving for your wedding, a new car, a down payment on a home, a week at the beach, that new dining room set, or a family trip to an amusement park.

You'll still want to set guidelines around this account so that no one is using it as a personal slush fund. Touch base a few times a year about how you might want to use the money so that you can be on the same page about building up how much you'll need. If you're planning for a known expense, like your family vacation, and you'll have the money set aside a few months in advance (maybe your bonus in January covers vacation in July), you could consider giving it a boost by investing in a CD for three or six months or placing it into a money market account. The interest might cover an extra activity you can all enjoy.

If your goal is a little further out, at least two years, then talk to your financial advisor about how to invest your savings for it. When interest begins compounding on your periodic contributions, the savings will grow with less effort on your part.

Getting all of this money into savings probably seems like an impossible task. Especially if one of you is recovering from the debt of divorce, death of a spouse, or the initiation of child support, it's hard to find anything left to save at the end of each month. Take your time building these accounts. Use bonuses from work or money earned from a second job to build it up. Review your cash flow and choose one weekly expense to give up and put into the cash reserve instead. Change your direct deposit instructions at work to have some money placed in savings right from your paycheck. By making it a set contribution that happens automatically, you'll get used to living on the amount that actually hits your main living expenses bank account. It takes effort, and sometimes it's really hard to set that money aside but having it there when you really need it makes all the difference.

One of my clients recently shared a story about a friend who was almost in serious trouble because she was without a cash reserve. The woman was negotiating her divorce, and her number one priority was to maintain ownership of her house so that her kids wouldn't have to move. She was able to keep the house, but it was re-financed without property taxes factored into the payments. She was well aware that she owed the property taxes, but she had no way to pay the lump sum as the due date loomed closer and closer. Self-employed in direct sales, she had taken an income hit during the divorce proceedings, and she didn't qualify for a loan. In the end, some very good friends stepped in to provide the needed funds, and she was spared the further expenses of property tax delinquency. You can bet that building up her savings was top of mind after that!

All of this work will set a firm foundation for building your blended family life. I recommend working with a trusted financial advisor to make sure that all of your bases get covered, that all of your decisions are clear to each other, and so that you can move forward together as a cohesive unit. Remember that you can download my resource guide on finding the right financial advisor for you by visiting the Resources section of this book.

SETTING UP HOUSE

Reviewing all the numbers at the table over a series of conversations is crucial for the next step, which is actually putting it all into practice.

I haven't been shy about the fact that I am a planner. Prior to our remarriage, I needed to work through all the information methodically, set goals, designate authorizations, run the calculations, and build up a nicely organized packet of our life on paper. That was all me —all planning.

That's not Jim, though. Jim put up with my planning to get to the part that's all him—all doing. See, I could have planned forever. I would have been plenty happy to sit down with a highlighter every night to decide how this would look "someday." Jim would have been happy to throw our lives together and start planning as we go. I appreciate that balance between us.

In our case, we really had hammered out all of the details. We had a trusted financial advisor, talked about the accounts, covered our values and plans for our kids, and compromised. It was time to apply all that planning into our next life phase together. As I mentioned earlier, we had our wedding date set. I was building my book of business to replace the income from my late husband's pension that I would lose in remarriage and to make sure we could get an affordable healthcare plan.

Just as everything seemed to be falling into place, the ground shifted quite a bit. Not only did the world shut down in 2020, but Jim's ex-wife was diagnosed with terminal cancer in 2021. Our agreed-upon financial plan was already in place as our foundation for making decisions, but we also had to recalibrate rather quickly.

This is the great thing about planning. You don't know the future; you can't know it. But you can prepare a whole lot of things in advance to be able to manage life's big surprises. When those surprises happen, you'll have an inventory of tools and trusted professionals ready to be put to work for whatever you need to do next.

Our recalibration was to go ahead and move everyone into my house ahead of schedule. Financially, it would help us reach the goals we had set. It would also allow us to consolidate our resources for supporting all of the kids in so many new dynamics. Since my office was right down the street and Jim's schedule was still very flexible, we figured pulling everyone under one roof would allow us to start navigating life as a blended family.

Now, it was the year 2020, and I had six kids under my roof. I was building my new practice while trying to be flexible with their schedules. All the kids were doing some online learning, so our cash flow worksheet needed a significant bump to the Wi-Fi line expense! One particular day, I remember walking home for lunch. All six kids, aged ten to eighteen, were home and trying to get through their school days in pretty much every room of the house.

As I got close to the house, I heard a goose honking. I thought, "What in the world is a goose doing around here?" Well, the goose got louder as I got close to home. So loud, in fact, that I discovered it was my very own goose. Only it wasn't a goose at all. It was Jim's youngest son, practicing his saxophone in the backyard because all the other kids had locked him out of the house!

Those were some tight quarters. But honestly, I'm truly grateful that we brought it all together the way we did. Saxophone blues jams on the patio aside, our kids got along really well, and everyone was gracious about making our blended family a happy one.

I credit our ability to shift gears in 2020 to the financial planning that Jim and I had already set in motion. With all the new facts on the ground, Jim and I reviewed our financial situation again. What could we do with what we had, and what did we need?

I was getting my financial practice off the ground, and Jim was again repositioning his career. He hung up his tool belt to help me grow the business (bless his soul). At that time, I fully understood exactly how much pressure my dad was under to keep his job when he was the sole income earner for our family. It's a heavy load when everyone depends on you for their ability to eat and sleep.

You might be under that pressure now—maybe even from more than one household. If you are supporting children in their other parents' home while also trying to create a safe and happy place for them with you, it may be suffocating at times. But it doesn't have to be like that for the rest of their childhood. That's why you're reading this book—to take steps now that will create more stability and freedom for your family.

ALL UNDER ONE ROOF

My blended family was not unique in that we faced a rushed timeline to get under one roof. Pandemics aside, when partners come together in a blending situation, there is often a good reason to start moving forward faster than expected. Sustaining multiple households with varying child schedules and support arrangements is a huge strain on time, finances, and emotions.

Almost all of my clients who are financially planning for a blended family will shorten their timeline during the process. The transportation schedule is hectic, too many rents or mortgages are being paid, dinners are always out because each house is too small to hold everyone, gas, and miles are getting out of control on the cars, someone is always missing the correct shoes for weather and activity, and one unexpected car repair or doctor bill always finally brings it all to a head.

Before you move in together, take stock of a few of these details:

- Will you have to travel a longer distance to pick up or deliver your household kids?
- Does the custody order stipulate changes to the pickup and drop-off schedule based on moving outside a certain radius, or might the other parent file a custody order change due to a greater distance?
- Will the move require any children to change school districts, and does this need to be addressed through the custody process?
- Will anyone have to travel farther for work, which will increase gas, toll, and maintenance expenses?
- Does your shared home need updates or improvements to accommodate your whole blended family?
- Can you consolidate membership accounts now that you're in the same household?

Only you and your partner can decide on cohabitating in a married or non-married state. This is not a decision for the children to make. It is not something that one partner's ex-spouse can stop. It's not up to your parents, domestic relations, friends, or coworkers. By all means, seek wise counsel from people you deeply respect and trust. Go ahead and ask me how it looks from a financial perspective! When all is said and done, you and your partner must move forward in the best manner for your relationship.

If marriage is an absolute must before you share an address, then get yourselves down to your local county offices and get hitched. Bring the people who are most meaningful to your union, say "I do," and then start packing.

You have truly come so far already. Your love is genuine, your commitment is real, and your dedication to your partner is steadfast.

If something is holding you back, look within to examine what it might be. Are you afraid to take that final step into full transparency and vulnerability with your partner? Are there past hurts and old baggage trying to stall this move? This is completely natural and normal. But the truth is that those things can hold you back forever if you let them. Address the real issues that still do need to be discussed. But recognize fear where it exists and conquer it. Trust your relationship, drop the extra burdens of living apart, and get your new blended household started.

One couple, both divorced with kids, made it clear to one another from the start that they had no interest in long-term dating. They had both been deeply hurt, and they only wanted to be in a fully committed relationship with someone they could trust. The woman was managing her property okay on her own, and she loved her house dearly, but it was a huge financial strain. The man had been renting a house, so he had no sentimental ties to a property. He was more than willing to move into her home. The catch is that they were both very strong in their faith and did not want to live together before marriage. They spent one whole winter getting to know each other well, and they were married by Easter! They got a few raised eyebrows about moving so quickly, but honestly, they had put in all the work to achieve their goal. They were honest with one another from day one, and it was a great match. Condensing their finances into one household wasn't the main priority. Still, the benefits of it allowed them to accelerate some property improvements that had been on the wife's dream list for a few years.

If you and your partner have been living apart during this financial planning phase, then most decisions still exist only on paper. True blending happens when you all come together under one roof and start managing daily, weekly, monthly, and long-term finances as a unit. Once you share your day-to-day space, you are really putting your financial plan into action.

BUILDING FAMILY RESILIENCE

You have your accounts worked out, know who pays what and how, and understand your cash flow. Living as a family is simply a matter of working within your financial plan and dealing with all kinds of unexpected surprises until they settle down as part of your normal rhythm of life.

We looked at our financial plan in light of the changes we had made with the pandemic. We were all in one house with Jim's kids, sharing their time between two households. We were still inching closer to our wedding day, but we had really solidified our partnership. Jim's decision to support my business over his carpentry trade both simplified and clarified our financial plan.

I asked Jim to join me in my financial planning practice as my "everything but" guy. His job would be to handle everything but the financial advising. He learned Microsoft Excel and started managing the calendar, planning events, buying swag, setting up meetings, and networking with me. I work directly with clients as a CERTIFIED FINANCIAL PLANNER™. We split the income in half so that we are always earning the same amount. The way I see it, we are a family business. Our family can't run without this business, and our business can't run without this family. He and I are in it together, earning every penny together.

All together, under one roof, we still had to feel our way through the day-to-day decisions. In our tabletop financial discussions, it was one thing to say that dinner out for all eight of us was probably doable every few weeks. Let me tell you that once you get the first bill for an eight-person (including teenage boys) dinner out, every few weeks turns into every few months pretty darn fast!

It's essential to remember that although you have created your blended home with all kinds of agreements and boundaries, financial disagreements will still pop up.

One client told me that her kids and step-kids had started resenting each other over Wawa. Wawa is a popular convenience store in Pennsylvania that makes great hoagies (subs to the rest of the world) precisely to your order. My client had sole custody of her kids, and she typically had dinner on the table every night. Her husband had a one-weeknight and every-other-weekend arrangement with his kids. During his weeknight pickup, he always stopped at Wawa with his kids to get hoagies for dinner. In his mind, that was the perfect tradition. His wife didn't have to hold up dinner for her kids while he was transporting his; his kids enjoyed the consistency of knowing their weekly dinner, and it was simply a nice thing to do together. What my client's kids saw, however, was that their stepsiblings got to bring hoagies home with their dad every week, and they didn't. The parents had no idea the kids were all under each other's skin about it until one night when suddenly, lettuce and pickles were flying through the air, and a hoagie went face down—*splat*—on the floor. All the kids were in tears. From that moment on, the whole family alternated with a hoagie night and a homecooked meal night each week.

If you think the kids don't notice when money is being spent, how much, and on whom, think again. They are paying attention, and they are forming opinions. They might not have the correct information, but when has that ever stopped us from making a judgment?

Get ahead of this the best you can by formulating a plan around spending money on or with the kids. Talk about things like:

- Allowance or getting paid for chores and house jobs
- Paying for clothes, toys, and treats
- Paying for hobbies, sports, camps, or music
- Buying or allowing the use of cars
- Factoring child support into how money is spent on a given child
- Saving for college or trade school
- Cosigning for education, auto, or home loans
- Aging out of allowance or contributing to their own expenses

As a couple, it is vital to review your spending practices frequently to ensure that the kids are treated fairly. Your definition of fair will vary by age, time spent in the home, child support orders, and other contributors. I caution against allowing it to go too far into the "your kids/my kids" breakdown of splitting expenses. The goal is to operate like a family, which means all the adults are doing their best to create a financially balanced home for all the kids.

PEOPLE ON THE OTHER SIDE OF THE DOOR

Your household kids won't be the only people noticing and forming opinions on how your blended family finances are managed. The other parents who make up your big picture will often seem to know plenty about your finances and will have some opinions, whether they share them directly with you or not. Other people could factor into your particular scenario as well. Think of families of deceased spouses, adult children, ex-in-laws, and maybe even half-siblings of kids in your blended family.

Here's the thing about all of those voices and ears and thoughts. You can keep all of those people on the other side of your door. But you might not be able to keep them from looking in the window or holding their ears up to the walls, and you can't control what the kids say when they join those folks out on the porch. All you can really do is manage your boundaries to the best of your ability, deal with the damage when it occurs, and accept that which is beyond your control.

I strongly encourage you and your partner to set boundaries as a couple regarding what you will discuss in front of or with the kids. Some families talk openly about various topics, while others can't tell you everyone's favorite color. You and your partner may come from different perspectives regarding what gets discussed with the kids. For the sake of your relationship as a couple, it is vital to be on the same page regarding what you are each comfortable sharing with the kids.

These are some questions to ponder while you figure out what works:

- What is age-appropriate?
- How much of what we say out loud gets reported to another household?
- Does money make one or more of our kids feel burdened, spoiled, entitled, or insecure?
- Are we manipulating the kids with money by offering it or withholding it conditionally?
- Is someone else manipulating the kids with money?
- Are the kids attempting to manipulate us with money, or are they lying about finances?
- Does it help the kids' relationships with each other to see fairness in spending?
- Do they or should they know how much money we make?
- Do they or should they know what is paid in child support and what is mandated over that amount?

You might have different answers for different kids, and that's fine. At the same time, you should never assume that the kids in your blended family will keep financial information confidential. Even if you ask them not to share something with a sibling, stepsibling, or other parent, money talk always seems to make its way out. This goes for what you directly tell them about finances and what they observe or experience.

Have you ever had an ex-spouse bring up a sizeable purchase you made as though they are making some kind of accusation? You didn't tell them about the purchase, and it doesn't have the slightest thing to do with them. That doesn't seem to matter. The insinuation is either that you are failing to provide for your child or that you are flaunting some high level of wealth to win favor in the child's eyes.

Generally speaking, what they relay has little more than a kernel of truth, but they built the story around it that worked for their purposes, and now you're in a position to defend your private financial decisions. If you have experienced this, you probably also noticed rather quickly that your child did not instigate any drama. Whether they simply chatted about the purchase or answered a direct question the other parent asked, they were not actively trying to pit anyone against the other. Of course, this isn't always the case. Kids are flawed humans just like us, and they do sometimes manipulate to achieve their own goals. In all cases, the point is to understand that your finances are probably being discussed on the other side of that door.

Knowing this fact and dealing with this fact are two separate things. Remember, you can only control what you do in your home. Sometimes your choice to maintain firm boundaries about financial topics will result in your household's children (or the other parent) having a wildly incorrect or imbalanced set of information. They might get all the numbers out of another house, but none out of yours. They might be kept up to date on income, child support amounts, cash flow, and the cost of goods in one home but not another. They might be told a narrative about your finances and decisions that has nothing to do with how you truly operate. However, you and your partner feel this needs to be dealt with in practice, talk about it now. And then do your darned best to stick to the rules you set.

That couple I mentioned earlier—the ones who chose to get married quickly—began hearing financial accusations from the start. Combining their households resulted in her ex-husband mentioning all the new electronics and bikes she had recently bought. There was absolutely nothing new. Her new husband added the contents of his house to hers, and most of his stuff was in excellent condition! Within a few weeks, she noticed that her ex-husband kept remarking on how he can't compete financially with all of her new husband's wealth. She could clearly see the pattern at play. Her kids would head to Dad's house and chat about what they had done during the week, usually using all the "new" stuff that had come into their house. Maybe they hooked up the bigger TV. Maybe they rode bikes with mom and step-dad. Maybe they played video games they had never tried before.

These are all everyday things that families do on an average day. Unfortunately, the ex-husband treated these benign activities as an act of flaunting on his ex-wife's part. Then, Dad discussed his perception of these financial disparities directly with the kids. What were mom and stepdad to do? They agreed to set a boundary. The financial issues that Dad was bringing up were irrelevant to the court-ordered child support allocation. Therefore, Mom saw no reason to respond to any of it. She didn't share anything her ex-husband said to her regarding money with the kids, and she did not ask them to keep anything private from him. She simply carried on running her household with her husband, and she didn't worry about what anyone else had to say about it.

This is the key to dealing with those on the other side of your door. If all they can do is talk, blame, accuse, and judge, they can't actually impact your financial reality. Don't allow fear, shame, guilt, or defensiveness to trick you into giving anyone power over your financial wellness. Remember, you cannot control what God does, what other people do, or what you do. You can only control what you do.

You might have to hear things you don't like. You might have to live with your household kids knowing true or false information about your finances. You might be manipulated into spending decisions that you don't feel are good. You might be the bad guy if you refuse to spend on something. You might have to bite your tongue so hard you're bleeding.

But ultimately, you and your partner *are* the only people in control of how you make and discuss your financial decisions.

READ THE LEGALESE

I've mentioned court-ordered child support several times, and I'd like to expand on that just a bit. First of all, I am not an attorney or qualified to give legal advice. But I do know the law regarding child support, and it is this: No one can waive a child's right to support.

Child support—as a matter of money to be paid by one party— often gets tossed into the divorce settlement discussions as though it's part of the bargaining process. It is not.

Child support is the money children have a right to receive for their living necessities. A total support amount is calculated using the incomes of both parents. Then, each parent's income and percentage of custody time determine their share of that total. Whoever owes more towards the allocation will pay that amount to the other parent. It's a math equation, plain and simple.

Do parents sometimes negotiate a reasonable amount outside the domestic relations system? Yes. But if that agreement comes under review at any time and it isn't enough per the calculator, the paying parent may owe arrears.

Please review the child support laws in your state and consult with a family law attorney to ensure you understand all the legalities. Don't ever try to play games with it. By that, I mean don't withhold child support payments to negotiate other matters with a child's other parent. And please, *please* don't ever keep a child from their other parent as a way of dealing with child support problems.

Some expenses that go above and beyond standard child support might be negotiable through domestic relations. Generally, both parents are responsible for financially covering a child's lifestyle. This means both parents might be court-ordered to share the cost of activity fees, music lessons, summer camps, and other extras. Make sure you understand exactly what you or the other parent are obligated to pay based on your child support order. It's common for activities that the kids participated in before their parents' separation to be spelled out in the order. Later, suppose one parent begins stacking up the activities with a blanket expectation that the other parent must help pay for them. In that case, it might be time to schedule a review to make sure any new expenses are affordable and reasonable.

If child support is being paid for multiple children, a review will be in order when each one ages out of the requirement. In most states, this is age eighteen or high school graduation, whichever comes later. Some states require child support payments to continue through college, so get familiar with the laws that apply to your situation. A child support order is often written as a total dollar amount paid for all the children covered under the order. This means that the amount does not change when the oldest ages out of the order because there is no mathematical allocation per child. The paying parent will need to request a review through domestic relations to recalculate the amount on the remaining number of children under the order.

If you or your partner receive a letter stating that the child support amount will remain the same after someone graduates, that might not be the final determination. The amount will most likely change after a review. The review will consider all of the current information for both parents and the new amount will be based on that. Check your state's domestic relations website to run a rough calculation ahead of time if you want to get an idea of what to expect.

Child support can be a really emotionally charged topic in blended family households. I understand why, but I always encourage my clients to drain their feelings out of it. It's a math equation. It's what the kids have a right to expect from the parents who share them. The less you allow yourself to feel anything at all regarding child support, the easier it will be to deal with that amount as a number in your cash flow.

HOUSING YOUR DOCUMENTS

One of the biggest lessons I learned in widowhood was document management. When my husband passed away, I needed to produce papers and get into all of our accounts pretty quickly. Since I handled a lot of our day to day finances, this was fairly manageable for me. As I began my career in financial planning, however, I realized that this is harder than it needs to be for most people.

In the messiness of life, we lose track of things. You left a job years ago and forgot about the 401(k) you had there. You paid off your car and remember the title coming in the mail, but the last image of it in your mind is on top of the always present mail pile on the kitchen counter. You see an automatic payment go out to your life insurance policy every month, but darned if you know what your policy even says. You changed pediatricians twice since your oldest was born, but you have all the previous doctors' numbers saved in your phone. Since you moved out of your marital home during the divorce, your ex-spouse has all the kids' original birth certificates.

If someone else in your household pays the bills, manages the credit cards, keeps track of your Turnpike transponder, and logs in to your streaming services, would you be able to get access to all those accounts and passwords if that person is suddenly incapacitated? Would someone else be able to get into your accounts if you are suddenly unable to?

Document management is a basic life necessity that far too many of us ignore. Whether you live alone or with other people, someone has to be able to find your stuff. Not only that, but they also have to know what to do with it all. A document locator is a simple, detailed workbook that helps your designated people manage your affairs if you are either incapacitated or deceased. When I went through my first year of widowhood and learned about all the documents that I needed to gather for settling my late husband's affairs, I made a big fat file of all of them. Once I transitioned into my career as a financial planner, I turned my list into a resource for my clients and anyone else who would like it. You can download a free Document Locator by visiting the Resources section of this book.

Most of the documents listed in this workbook should look familiar. You already pulled out just about every file and account during your financial discussions with your partner. Now is a great time to organize all of your paperwork into an alphabetic filing system that someone can pick up to manage your affairs. When clients go through the onboarding process in our practice, they get access to an online portal that has a document vault section, pretty much like an online filing cabinet!

Even though you have theoretically already reviewed all of your accounts, this process is an opportunity for a double check on things. Did you remember to change your beneficiary on that rolled over IRA? Did you ever get around to notarizing the addendum to your will that names your partner as guardian of your minor children? Is that password that was caught up in a data breach deleted from all of your accounts? Do you have any new paperwork like a marriage certificate, updated social security card, or car insurance?

The documents you should gather and organize include:

- Appliances, Electronics, and Heavy Equipment

- Automobile—title, financing, insurance, warranty
- Bank Accounts
- Brokerage Investments
- Credit Cards
- Education
- Essential Documents—birth & marriage certificates, divorce decree, social security card
- Estate Documents
- Health Insurance
- Life Insurance
- Military Paperwork and Contacts
- Mortgage or Lease
- Medical
- Pets
- Prenuptial or Postnuptial Agreements
- Retirement Investments
- Taxes
- Utilities and Household Expenses

Use the Document Locator workbook to share additional information, such as names, phone numbers, usernames, and passwords, that your designated person would need to view or control all of these accounts and directives.

You and your partner should choose the individuals who will manage your affairs if you are both taken out of commission at the same time. Whether you have one person to handle both of your arrangements, or you have separate contacts lined up, make sure all the key players know about each other. They should know the hierarchy of authority, where to locate the information that will get them started, and which professionals can help them first. Consider telling the older kids who those people are as well.

LIVING AS A FAMILY

In my first book, I charted a timeline along the first three years of widowhood. There are many milestones and firsts that a widowed spouse must cross, and they are pretty identifiable. Blended families will have some noticeable milestones, such as first birthdays, holidays, vacations, and anniversaries. However, many blended milestones will be easier to identify after you have passed them. You might notice certain traditions taking shape, like Friday night movies together. Or maybe you'll realize that the kids got through their first territorial battle over the bathroom schedule and actually worked it out together.

The first time a stepmom is approved for transporting a kid to sports, a friend's house, or even the other parent's house might be a really big deal. When kids appeal to stepdad to persuade mom, ask him for advice, or hug him with genuine affection, it's a sign that a family system is in place. There is security in those relationships when stepsiblings start conspiring in the home, socializing in public, or giving each other pet names.

All of these things take time, grace, and patience. Building relationships among people who have been hurt and who have a lot of scar tissue is hard work. It can't be forced or manipulated, and it doesn't always happen at all. Sometimes personalities are incompatible. Sometimes outside influences are too strong. Sometimes the best you can hope for is mutual tolerance and minimal conflict.

The goal for your blended family should be harmony, even if you can't fully achieve it. If you are experiencing conflict, try to step back and really evaluate root causes. Kids might still be grieving the death of a parent or their parents' divorce. Outside voices might be manipulating or influencing opinions and perspectives. There might be a power struggle based on who lived in the house first or who lives in the house more often. There might be jealousy about the various relationships in the family.

You and your partner should privately discuss these issues with the goal of resolving them. Like all of our financial discussion preparation, try to keep your emotions and judgments to a minimum. You're on the same team working towards a unified solution. You can win together or lose together. If only one of you wins, you both lose.

Some of your options for resolving household conflict and nurturing harmony include:

- Family counseling with someone experienced in blended family systems;
- Focused planning of enjoyable activities and opportunities to get to know each other better;
- Individual attention for each child with their natural parent and stepparent;
- Seeking out shared interests and hobbies;
- Relocating to a new home that is a fresh start for the whole family; or
- Adopting a family pet who will be loved by all.

Our blended family was fortunate to be a pretty congenial bunch. All the kids got along well, and both Jim and I got along with each other's kids very well. Jim and his kids had moved into the house that my kids and I had lived in for several years, resulting in mostly good-natured power plays among the kids. My kids would claim bathroom privileges or say the TV was theirs. My kids were also older than Jim's, so that played a part. While it could get a little tense at times, we really did have a decent system. Then we got the news that Jim's ex-wife was at the end of her treatment possibilities and would be starting hospice care. Our house was in the neighboring school district, which meant that when she passed away, Jim's kids would immediately have to transfer out of their schools. This was a trauma we felt they could be spared in light of the one they couldn't.

My youngest was a senior, and it was January. We had satisfied the requirements for him to graduate in his current school district, even if he moved outside of it. That was all we needed to know to make our next move. We got married in June. By January, we were house hunting in Jim's kids' district. We found an absolute money pit of a foreclosure and settled as fast as we could. The new home we all entered as a blended family put everyone on equal footing in terms of ownership. It was no longer "our" house that "they" had moved into. It was all of ours, and it was a giant mess. To promote the kids' relationships and comfort in the house, Jim got to work on their bedrooms and creating a full family living space first. Our master bedroom was last on the list, and it's still not done!

This new home took our family unity to a whole new level. Our kids all share something special anyway, but it was kind of a big ask for my kids to move again. The house we were leaving was where they finally established a home of their own after their dad died. But they had amazing compassion for their stepsiblings. Having been through the death of a parent themselves, it was a no-brainer to them. If moving so that the younger kids could stay in the schools they knew and loved was what they had to do, they would do it. I'm really proud of all of our kids for how they cared for each other through that ordeal and how it has brought them all closer together.

Moving to a new house might not be an option for your blended family. But I would encourage you to think about your home life with an eye on family unity. Perhaps switching around the living spaces or bedrooms or remodeling to a style that fits everyone's taste could be enough to make everyone feel like your blended house is their own home. Speak to your financial advisor about what you can afford or plan for to resolve some of the conflicts and disruptions in your household.

We had to make several money decisions to transition to that foreclosure house. It meant yet another career shift for Jim (seriously, bless his soul). We felt the most economical choice was to have him work on the house to get it up to our living standards. But that meant taking him away from our financial practice. We filled in his duties with office staff, which, of course, added to our payroll expenses. We needed to adjust both our business and family spending plans, review life insurance policies based on changes in our roles, and make a few cuts. Keep in mind that we did all of this in about six months!

If you and your partner are about to change your living situation, you absolutely need to plan for it financially. But if you are already working with a solid financial plan and advisor, you can make your moves really quickly. Once again, this is the beauty of planning. When things get shaken up, and they always get shaken up, you aren't going to be starting from scratch to deal with them. Call your financial professional, tell them what's changing, and start evaluating your options. Not only will you be relieved that you're more prepared than you expected to be, but you'll be able to move forward as quickly or slowly as you need to.

THE RHYTHM OF YOUR
BLENDED HOME

ONCE YOU HAVE BEEN LIVING AS A BLENDED FAMILY FOR A while, you will discover your rhythm of life. It will continue to be unpredictable at times, but that's the reality for every family. Change is constant, but I believe in your ability to thrive in a changing environment.

Once you have your systems in place, it's important to revisit them at least annually. Come back to that financial table every year to debrief and to plan ahead.

REVIEW CASH FLOW

Pull out all of those cash flow supporting documents and review how your spending went over the past year:

- Did you pretty much stick to your spending plan?
- Were there unexpected expenses that you should have foreseen?
- Is your day-to-day spending pretty fair to the household?
- Did you come in way under on a few expenses?

Review your spending expectations for the coming year next:

- What changes are coming up this year that require spending or saving adjustments?
- Is it time to schedule the honeymoon you delayed, an anniversary trip, or a blended family vacation?
- If this is the year that you'll have all the kids for an important holiday, should you save for something extravagant?
- Is child support due for a review (check your state's review cycle), or will one of the kids be aging out?
- Will a custody arrangement change, or can you afford to pursue a custody change?
- Do you need to increase savings for house repairs, new appliances, a car, or education?
- Will your healthcare deductions change, including Flexible or Health Savings Account contributions?
- Will your retirement plan contributions automatically increase, or can you elect an increase?
- Is your grocery bill about to explode or shrink due to your kids becoming teenagers or moving out of the house?
- Are you planning to grow your family with more children?
- Will you buy a pet this coming year?
- Are any kids heading off to college?

REVIEW NET WORTH AND IMPORTANT DOCUMENTS

I recommend sitting down with your financial advisor once a year as well to review your net worth and future plans. It may be wise to adjust your investment mix, put some excess savings into an interest-bearing account, or take a distribution for a planned expense. When you sit down with your advisor, look at all of your beneficiary designations again. If the oldest kid is now the person you both feel should handle your affairs, it might be time to replace your current designations. The same goes for your will and estate documents. If the oldest child is an adult who you trust to care for minor children, change your guardianship directive.

I have a client whose step-kids were in high school when she had her own children. She had originally assumed that her step-kids should be the guardians of their siblings, but she and her husband decided to hold off on that designation until the oldest was at least thirty. Instead, they asked good friends who went to their church and had just adopted a baby to be their designated guardians. They instinctively felt as though that family would give their boys almost the same lifestyle through the rest of childhood. It would also allow young adult kids to establish themselves without the pressure of raising their younger siblings. Their plan is to revisit the designations once the older kids are over thirty and their younger boys are teenagers. At that point, it might make more sense to have the older siblings take guardianship and manage the trust for the younger boys through their final years of childhood.

When determining guardianship for minor children, it's important to think long and hard about whether their adult siblings (full, half, or step) are appropriate for the designation. Although by then you'll be dead and won't have a say anymore, you should take time to consider how other parents, ex-in-laws, and other siblings might play a role in their lives from that point forward. If you're uncomfortable with that possibility, a member of your own family or a friend might be better suited for the role of guardian.

Your will and estate documents do not just cover guardianship of the kids. You should review these documents every one-to-three years to make sure they are consistent with your current circumstances and wishes. As the kids get older, you might want to change the terms of your trust or consider whether or not you still need one. As you and your spouse get older and as your net worth grows, you might want to make new financial decisions for tax planning purposes.

Should you change your life insurance beneficiaries once the kids of your blended household are all adults? A parent might designate the other parent as a life insurance beneficiary since that's who would have sole custody of their shared children upon death. Or, maybe they will designate their own sibling or good friend as the beneficiary in order to protect their current partner from lawfare tactics the ex-spouse might use in pursuit of the estate's assets. When these issues resolve themselves because the kids are grown, make those updates to ensure that your money goes where you intend it to go.

Are your life insurance policies still the right coverage for your circumstances? Jim gives me a hard time about this, but I have a life insurance policy on him because of our money pit foreclosure house. He's the one putting all the labor into this house to get it up to our livable standards. If he falls off a ladder tomorrow, the kids and I will still need to finish the house! That life insurance policy covers the cost of hiring a contractor to finish the work on the house if Jim is suddenly incapacitated. When the house is complete, I can terminate that specific policy. My life insurance policy is intended to cover the costs and taxes of our home so that Jim and the kids will have that protection if I should pass away. We will probably keep that policy current for several more years. If your own policies are getting close to their term date, you'll need to review the renewal costs and your various options with your life insurance agent.

While you have your insurance agent's ear, request a review of your home and auto policies. Are you paying the best rates? Are you eligible for any new discounts? Did you remember to remove the oldest kid from your policies when they got their own apartment? Did you make home improvements that increase your home's value? Are you about to add new drivers to your household? Are kids about to move out and branch off to their own policies?

As the kids of your blended family reach adulthood, you may or may not want to begin including them in financial planning discussions. Some couples like to keep this topic fully private for their entire lives, while others prefer to start widening the circle to inform or involve their heirs. Discuss it as a couple first and come to an agreement about how much you will share and to whom.

REVISIT LONG-TERM PLANNING

There might be several years early in your blended family that you spend recovering from financial losses and complications. Your financial outlook should drastically improve as you resolve these matters over time. When it does, you and your partner might find yourselves daring to dream bigger than you once thought possible.

The long-term plans for your empty nest years and retirement lifestyle are likely to change as you move closer to them. As a result, many of your other financial plans could change. I mentioned earlier that I plan to pass my house down to my kids as their share of their dad's inheritance. That's still the case even in the money pit foreclosure we moved to after we got married. Jim will never be kicked out of that house if I die before him, but when he does leave it, my kids will be able to sell it and split the proceeds. That decision has been in place for several years, and it was an important element of my prenup with Jim. But that doesn't mean it has to be permanent. If we're able to provide a comparable financial inheritance to my kids through some other means, such as investments or other properties, then Jim and I can visit the lawyer to revise all the paperwork. If you and your partner wrote a prenup, postnup, or addendums to your wills, you have the right to make changes over time.

One couple I work with decided to get married once all their kids had gone through college. His late wife had been a federal employee, so he wanted to collect that pension for as long as possible. He could remarry without penalty or losing his pension and benefits at a certain age. In addition, they wanted the kids to have the most favorable financial aid outcomes when they completed FAFSA. The oldest child had just started high school when they made this decision. Of all four of their blended household kids, only one decided to go to college. The youngest two actually enlisted in the military right out of high school.

At that point, they didn't financially need the pension as income. They also felt like their relationship was not as strong as it could be, and they had put off the security of marriage longer than either of them really ever wanted to. What they had initially thought was the right practical decision was turning out to be an emotional strain on both of them. They called to let me know they went ahead and got married about four years ahead of schedule, and they couldn't be happier. We scheduled an appointment to get all of their documents updated right away.

The decisions you and your partner are making today are based on your combined history up until now. You can only plan for a hypothetical future, so hold those plans loosely. As your circumstances change, be open to changing your spending plan, long-term plans, retirement goals, and inheritance intentions.

MAINTAINING HEALTHY RELATIONSHIPS AND BOUNDARIES

In the previous chapter, I mentioned the people on the "other side of the door" of your blended household. I didn't mention the people who might be invited into your living room pretty regularly. I should note that sometimes the very same people will be in both groups.

The people in your living room are family members, good friends, and, yes, sometimes, individuals involved in one of your prior families. These people might be your trusted confidants. Or they might *want* to be your trusted confidants. They might be someone you confide in, but your partner does not, and vice versa. They might be adult children who were once part of your blended household or maybe who were already launched adults when you blended your family.

As a widow, mom, stepmom, financial professional, and someone who wants the best for your relationship, I desperately urge you to practice healthy boundaries in all of these relationships. The one relationship that requires full trust and honesty is the one you have with your partner. When others get involved in the private details of that relationship, you and your partner may be impacted by the opinions, actions, and overreactions of others. Your relationship could be left with some permanent consequences as a result.

We all need people to confide in. That's natural. My chief concern is that when the people you choose to confide in have any ability at all to use your information against you, against your partner, or for their own gain, it puts you in a vulnerable position.

With my widow clients, I call this the "brother-in-law rule." Many of my widowed clients have a brother-in-law or some similar type of friend or family member who turns up out of nowhere, claiming to be a savvy financial expert. He (or she) ends up with too much information and too much decision-making power, usually to the detriment of my client's financial wellness.

When you or your partner discuss private relationship matters— whether related to finances, the kids, the court system, ex-families, or your love life—with people closely connected to your family, there is a potential for negative effects.

Sometimes, one member of the couple even speaks to their ex-spouse about the current relationship! As odd as that seems at first glance, it's not all that uncommon. Not all divorces are nasty; sometimes the exes continue to get along on a lot of matters. Despite no longer being married, they still have a level of familiarity that makes conversation easy.

During my earliest days of widowhood, I relied heavily on one of my late husband's sisters to help me through some of the paperwork and financial decisions. Despite her absolute discretion to this very day, I still find it unsettling that someone knows so many details about my financial situation. Will she view my decisions for my kids through the lens of knowing exactly how much money there was on that one day? She probably won't, of course. But the fact that I think about it often is a good reason to caution my clients about what information they share and to whom.

It's not all about making rigid boundaries, though. Jim and I are unique in that we are the only remaining parents for all six of our kids. I committed to keeping my late husband's family in my kids' lives from the very start. When Jim's ex-wife passed away, he extended the olive branch to her family to put them at ease and reassure them that they would be included in all of our lives. They are invited to share in many family events like proms, Thanksgiving dinners, pierogi-making days, and casual get-togethers.

In a totally bizarre—but completely normal for us—turn of events, Jim and I became integral to the healing process for his ex-wife's siblings. We got really silly and started opening up our money pit mess of a foreclosure to the other sides of our kids' families every Sunday. Through those visits, my former in-laws became a valuable support system for Jim's ex-family. They began to connect on grieving a sibling, and we got to watch some very caring relationships form out of that.

I know that we are both fortunate to have these positive relationships among the other members of our kids' families. We are careful of the boundaries and protecting our own marriage, as well as the dynamics of our blended family. We keep in mind that by inviting all these folks into our living room, they are in a position to see some of our lives and form opinions based on their first loyalties. We're okay with this. Jim and I have achieved a level of trust and security in our relationship that prevents us from dwelling on what others might think.

I encourage you and your partner to put in the work to navigate these relationships as well. If you can manage to foster positivity among the ex-families for the sake of your blended household kids, you will benefit as a family. Sometimes, this isn't easy, especially if goodwill is not reciprocated towards your blended family. Try not to engage in any hostilities. Be pleasant, make space for your household kids to feel comfortable talking about or spending time with other members of their family, and practice grace. Your blended household kids will remember how the adults in their lives treated or talked about the people they love.

My current generation of millennial clients are heavily impacted by divorced childhoods. The scar tissue they bring to the financial table is very thick. They are dealing with serious trust issues regarding family alienation and money that make their current relationships difficult to navigate. When someone is raised in a home where language and money are used as weapons to interfere with parent-child relationships, they struggle to see every relationship as anything other than a transaction. I'm not a counselor, but I put in a lot of time helping these clients form a more positive relationship with finances and their life partner. But when they bring up the financial requests and pressure their aging parents are beginning to put on them now? Ha! They remember who gave them those scars, and they aren't rushing to offer that kind of support.

If you are one of those former kids carrying the scars of angry divorced parents, I'm sorry for the pain you experienced. It's not fair that your parents placed you in the middle of their drama, made you pick sides, made you uncomfortable for loving your own family members, or burdened you with financial information that wasn't yours to know. I challenge you to break that cycle in your own blended family. Let the kids be kids whenever they are under your roof, and don't be afraid to reassure them that they do not need to carry the burdens of any adults in their lives.

FINANCIAL CONSIDERATIONS OF THE SANDWICH GENERATION

Speaking of aging parents, you or your partner could very well be dealing with the effects of being in the sandwich generation. While you're busy navigating the financial issues of being a blended household, your parents might be trying to hop into the mix. My mother went through a gray divorce when I started dating Jim, and boy, was that interesting!

Discuss the potential for taking financial responsibility for either of your parents with one another and with your financial advisor. If having to care for a parent is a possibility, then get in front of it with some serious discussions with that person. Talk about long-term care insurance, retirement home plans, powers of attorney, and healthcare directives. If one of your parents intends for you to be their caregiver at some point in the near or far future, you need to know about it. Remember that these conversations should be handled with as much compassion and respect as possible. The current population of aging seniors—as a generation—tend to be very self-sufficient individualists who aren't accustomed to asking for help. Start these questions from a place of curiosity or by saying you want to make sure you can advocate for what they actually want if they can't speak for themselves. If they understand that you intend to carry out their wishes rather than your own or a doctor's, it should be easier for them to share their thoughts.

I mentioned earlier that many couples prefer to keep their financial information private indefinitely. While this is a choice that people have the right to make, it tends to make things complicated for those who will manage their affairs before and after their passing. If you or your partner are dealing with aging family members who need help, but who are unwilling to share information about their resources, you are not alone. Your financial advisor might be able to offer some additional strategies that help you navigate the important questions, or they might have a referral for a professional whose specialty is financial planning for elderly clients. Remember to use my resource to find a financial advisor to help you through this interview process, which you can download via the link in the Resources section of this book.

If you absolutely cannot get to the bottom of your elderly loved one's financial plan for late-in-life care, consider making your own contingency plan. You have your rainy day fund of three-to-six months of living expenses. Can you pour another month or two into that account? This would ensure you have cash on hand if you need to take time off of work, pay for short-term emergency care, or cover some medical expenses while the paperwork gets sorted out. As I mentioned before, you cannot control what other people do. You can only control what you do. Financial preparation can help you manage an aging parent's health decline in a way that allows you to focus on the relationship rather than the expenses.

ENJOY THE RIDE

We have covered a lot of ground over these pages. Blending a family is not for wimps; that's for sure! The fact is, you decided to pick up this book and start reading because you want your relationship to work.

You have concerns about all the complexities of a blended family relationship, and you know the uncomfortable statistics. You also really love your partner. If you didn't, you never would have gotten this far—either in your relationship or in this book. The actual quality of your personal relationship is a far more valid measure of success than all the combined statistical data in the world. You and your partner are capable of living a long, healthy, and joyful life together as a couple because you are willing to let each other behind your walls, speak openly and honestly about all the things, and extend a whole lot of grace each other's way.

You don't have to tell me that blended relationships are built on a foundation of pain. People are coming together from a place of hurt in 100% of all blended families. There is no other possibility. Someone or something has died, and we are broken because of it.

Blended relationships are also built on hope. Even in grief, trauma, pain, and suffering, humans have capacity for hope and a desire to love and live. We are resilient. *You* are resilient. You might not be the one entering your relationship from that place of brokenness, but you will share in the pain of those you love, nevertheless. That's part of love. Love and pain go hand in hand.

My goal for you is to harness your and your partner's capacity for resilience and direct it into strength. You each have individual strengths that will contribute to your financial and relational health. But more than that, you have strengths as a couple that no other two people can share. When you work together from these strengths, you have the potential to overcome all of your existing obstacles and meet each future challenge with confidence and clear heads.

I encourage you to dream big, strategize your long-term future, and plan your near future carefully (with professional help, please). Be honest with one another, earn trust, release bitterness and judgment, and forge a bond around your shared commitment. Fiercely advocate for each other, your household kids, and your relationship. Protect your home and the people in it, but don't close yourselves off to the wider community. Find your blended family's tribe, build new friendship circles, create traditions, and learn to love each other in special and unique ways.

When my blended family clients and I are ready to print their financial plan, which is really only complete for that very short moment in time, I encourage them to write a eulogy of sorts for their relationship. We've got this relationship all set up on the right track. You're on the same team, working towards the same goals, and you're prepared to win together. What does winning really look like? When you get to the end of your lives—your very long, happy lives—what do you want your household heirs to say about you at your funerals?

What are the attributes you hope they share about each of you? What do you hope they say about your relationship and how you loved one another and them as kids? Will they be proud of you? Will they be grateful for the legacy you've given them to carry forward? Are they happy with the allocation structure and tax consequences of their inheritance? Ha! That one is just a little financial planning humor; indulge me.

Think about how you want to be remembered as individuals and as a couple. Work backward from there to create the relationship that will leave that legacy.

A MESSAGE FROM ME TO YOU

I'VE SHARED WITH YOU MY HEART AND HARD-EARNED wisdom over these many pages. My current career began when I decided to become the person I needed most. As my circumstances changed, I evolved my focus and business to ensure I could keep being a valuable resource to the people walking similar paths to mine. I have been through some really messy things, and I know you have, too. I hope you have found reassurance from this resource that your mess is manageable, that your relationship can be very successful, and that your fears and frustrations are valid.

I want you to have the confidence to know that when we move forward into what might feel scary or uncomfortable, we grow, and our relationship blossoms. That growth improves the lives around us. I want you to know that I'm here for you. I'm a safe person who doesn't judge that momentary resentment or snark because I know you've got to release it somewhere. I hope you can picture me next to you, cheering on your relationship and encouraging you to go the distance. I hope you can also hear my voice reminding you that you've got to get those numbers on the table so that you and your partner can truly come together to chart your financial future for your blended household.

If you need more from me, please don't hesitate to reach out! Find me at www.donnajeankendrick.com/book to download my resources, listen to my podcast (where you'll meet Jim!), and learn more about navigating all kinds of life transitions. I'd love to connect personally as well! Email me directly at hello@donnajeankendrick.com or search on LinkedIn for Donna Jean Kendrick, CFP®, CDFA®.

In closing, I leave you with this advice, "Enjoy the moments. Enjoy where you are, where you've been, and where you're going."

GLOSSARY

ASSETS
An asset is any resource of value, tangible or intangible, that is owned by an individual, a company, or a government with the expectation that it will provide an economic benefit. This would be things like your house, rental property, retirement savings accounts, art, stocks, etc. Link to a guide on assets and liabilities: https://www.thebalance.com/a-guide-to-assets-and-liabilities-5197387

BONDS
A bond is a fixed-income instrument that represents a loan made by an investor to a borrower (typically corporate or governmental). It could be thought of as an I.O.U. between the lender and borrower, which includes the details of the loan and its payments. Companies, municipalities, states, and sovereign governments use bonds to finance projects and operations. Bond owners are debtholders, or creditors, of the issuer.

CASH RESERVE
Funds should be set aside for use in emergency situations, the unexpected. For single-income families, the goal is six months of expected

costs. For reliable two-income families, the goal is three months of costs. Cash reserves should be kept in liquid accounts such as savings, money markets, or CDs.

On the morning of my wedding day to Greg, my aunt pulled me aside before walking down the aisle. She asked me if I had a secret account, an account that Greg didn't know about, that I could put a percentage of each paycheck into, from both his and my paycheck, so that if there was an emergency, the money could be there. My uncle was a blue-collar worker in Philadelphia at the sugar plant, and when it closed down, she used the funds from that secret account to feed their five kids and pay the mortgage. In my practice, currently, I call this your cash reserve or rainy day fund. And the answer is yes. Yes, I did have that account, and it covered the mortgage for the first two months after Greg's loss. And yes, when my aunt walked through the visitation line before Greg's funeral service, she checked in to make sure I had my rainy day fund ready to go.

COBRA
The Consolidated Omnibus Budget Reconciliation Act (COBRA) gives workers and their families who lose their health benefits the right to choose to continue group health benefits provided by their group health plan for limited periods of time under certain circumstances such as voluntary or involuntary job loss, reduction in the hours worked, transition between jobs, death, divorce, and other life events. Qualified individuals may be required to pay the entire premium for coverage up to 102% of the cost of the plan.

COMMISSIONS
Typically, a commission is compensation for buying or selling a financial asset, such as a stock.

CONFLICTS OF INTEREST

When an advisor's interests (including the interests of their firm) are adverse to the advisor's duty to the client, or when an advisor has duties to one client that are adverse to another client.

EQUITIES

Equity is the portion of a business or other asset that belongs to its owners. It is calculated by taking the total value of the asset and subtracting any outstanding liabilities, like bills and taxes. It can be found on most companies' balance sheets and is used to determine their health. Equity can be split among multiple owners, the same way big companies often have many shareholders. Most of your investments that you want to grow will be in equities, and there are many different types, for example, Large Cap Value, Large Cap Growth, Small Cap, International, and Emerging Markets. During your investment portfolio review, as your financial profession, to help you understand asset classes and the role equities play.

EXCHANGE-TRADED FUNDS (ETF)

An exchange-traded fund, or ETF, is a fund that can be traded on an exchange like a stock, meaning it can be bought and sold throughout the day. ETFs often have lower fees than other types of funds.

Depending on the type, ETFs have varying levels of risk. ETFs can sometimes look and feel like mutual funds but are used differently within your portfolio, either to lower costs, model an index, or help with tactical opportunities. Your financial professional should share the role an ETF plays in the portfolio they are managing for you.

FEES

There are different types of fees that a financial advisor might charge: You may pay a fee based on a percentage of the investable assets the financial advisor manages for you. You may pay an hourly rate or a fixed fee for the service. You may also be able to pay a monthly or quarterly retainer fee (also known as a subscription fee) for the services of a CFP® professional on an ongoing basis.

FINANCIAL PLAN
The output of a collaborative process between client and advisor helps maximize a client's potential for meeting their individual life goals. The plan provides financial advice that integrates relevant elements of the client's personal and financial circumstances.

FIXED INCOME
An income from a pension or investment that is set at a particular figure and does not vary (as a dividend) or rise with the rate of inflation.

INVESTABLE ASSETS
Liquid and near-liquid assets include cash, checking and savings accounts, stocks, bonds, and mutual funds, and retirement accounts, and trusts. Some advisors earn fees based on a percentage of the investable assets they manage for you.

LIABILITIES
Broadly speaking, liabilities are things like credit card debts, mort-gages, and personal loans. A liability is a debt you must pay off, now or in the future. Link to a guide on assets and liabilities: https://www. thebalance.com/a-guide-to-assets-and-liabilities-5197387

NET WORTH
Net worth is a measure of wealth. It is the sum of all assets owned by a person or a company minus any obligations or liabilities.

MUTUAL FUND
A mutual fund is a type of financial vehicle made up of a pool of money collected from many investors to invest in securities like stocks, bonds, money market instruments, and other assets. Mutual funds are operated by professional money managers, who allocate the

fund's assets and attempt to produce capital gains or income for the fund's investors. A mutual fund's portfolio is structured and maintained to match the investment objectives stated in its prospectus.

NONQUALIFIED
Non-qualified investments are accounts that do not receive preferential tax treatment. You can invest as much or as little as you want in any given year and withdraw at any time. Money that you invest into a non-qualified account is money that you've already received through income sources and paid income tax on.

PROBATE
Probate is the legal process of reviewing a will to determine whether it is valid and authentic. It also refers to the general administration of a deceased person's will or the estate of a deceased person without a will.

QUALIFIED FUNDS
Qualified money refers to money in retirement accounts, such as IRAs, 401(k)s, and 403(b)s. ERISA, or the Employee Retirement Income Security Act, invented qualified money. Before 1974, the only retirement accounts that existed were pensions.

RESTRICTED STOCK UNITS (RSU)
Restricted stock units (RSUs) refer to an agreement by a company to issue an employee shares of stock or the cash value of shares of stock on a future date. Each unit represents one share of stock or the cash value of one share of stock that the employee will receive in the future.

STOCKS
A stock (also known as equity) is a security that represents the ownership of a fraction of a corporation. This entitles the owner of the stock to a proportion of the corporation's assets and profits equal to how much stock they own. Units of stock are called "shares."

TAX-DEFERRED

Tax-deferred status refers to investment earnings that accumulate tax-free until the investor constructively receives the gain, Such as Traditional IRA savings or 401(k) contributions.

TAX-FREE

Tax-free refers to certain types of goods and financial securities (such as municipal bonds) that are not taxed. The tax-free status of these goods, investments, and income may incentivize individuals and business entities to increase spending or investing, resulting in economic stimulus (e.g., ROTH IRA).

RESOURCES

Remember that you are stronger than you think.

— DONNA JEAN KENDRICK

Navigating blending a family can feel overwhelming, but you don't have to do it alone. I've compiled a collection of essential resources designed to support and guide you through the first three years of this journey. These are the resources I've mentioned throughout the book.

- Download resources at www.donnajeankendrick.com/Books

OTHER EXTERNAL RESOURCES

- **Credit Review:** www.annualcreditreport.com

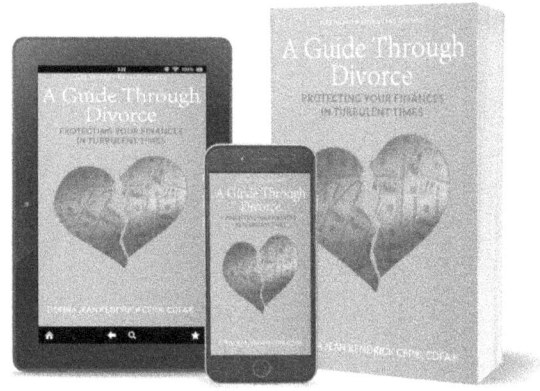

ABOUT THE AUTHOR

Donna Jean Kendrick's life transformed when she blended her family with Jim's, creating a bustling household of six children. As the founder of Sephton Financial, she already specialized in supporting families through significant transitions such as widowhood and divorce. However, her own experience of remarriage and blending families deeply

Photo credit: Sarah Miller

enriched her understanding and fueled her passion for helping others navigate similar challenges.

After the sudden death of her first husband, Greg, when she was just forty years old, Donna faced the daunting task of securing her family's financial future while managing her grief and supporting her three young children. This profound personal challenge revealed her calling: to assist families in transition to ensure they feel financially secure and supported.

With Jim, Donna found love again and encountered the complex realities of merging two families with distinct needs and financial implications. This journey inspired her to write *A Guide for Blended Families*, where she leverages her professional expertise and personal insights to help others smoothly combine their lives and finances. In this guide, Donna provides practical advice, empathetic stories, and actionable steps to empower families to thrive together in their new configurations. Learn more at www.donnajeankendrick.com.

ABOUT THE PUBLISHER

Founded in 2019, Highlander Press is a vibrant, mid-sized publishing house dedicated to transforming the world through the power of words. We are deeply committed to diversity and bringing big ideas to the forefront. At Highlander Press, we help authors navigate the journey from initial concept through writing, editing, and publishing, culminating in the release of a book that not only fulfills a lifelong dream but also solidifies their expertise and boosts their confidence.

Our unique approach centers on forging strong, collaborative relationships with women-owned businesses across the publishing spectrum, including graphic design, marketing, launching, copyright management, and publicity. We believe in the power of community and operate by the mantra, "a rising tide lifts all boats." This philosophy not only enhances our business model but also ensures that our authors receive unparalleled support and opportunities to succeed.

Join us in making a mark in the literary world, where your voice is heard, and your message has the power to change lives.

www.ingramcontent.com/pod-product-compliance
Lightning Source LLC
Chambersburg PA
CBHW051638120626
46551CB00014B/2124